Here we go, one last time!
Willkommen beim letzten Band der *Wordmaster*-Reihe! Diesmal gibt es den *Wordmaster* im Doppelband, d. h. Access 5 und 6 zusammen.

Sobald du neue Wörter in der Schule besprochen hast, mach die **Words and phrases** in diesem Heft. Es gibt nun **keine deutsche Übersetzung** der Beispielsätze mehr. Du sollst die neuen Vokabeln vielmehr beim Lesen des Beispielsatzes erschließen. Wo dir das mal nicht gelingt, gibt es zur Hilfe eine Auswahl an deutschen Übersetzungen der gefragten Vokabeln. Das ist ein bisschen anspruchsvoller als bisher, macht die Sache aber auch spannender.

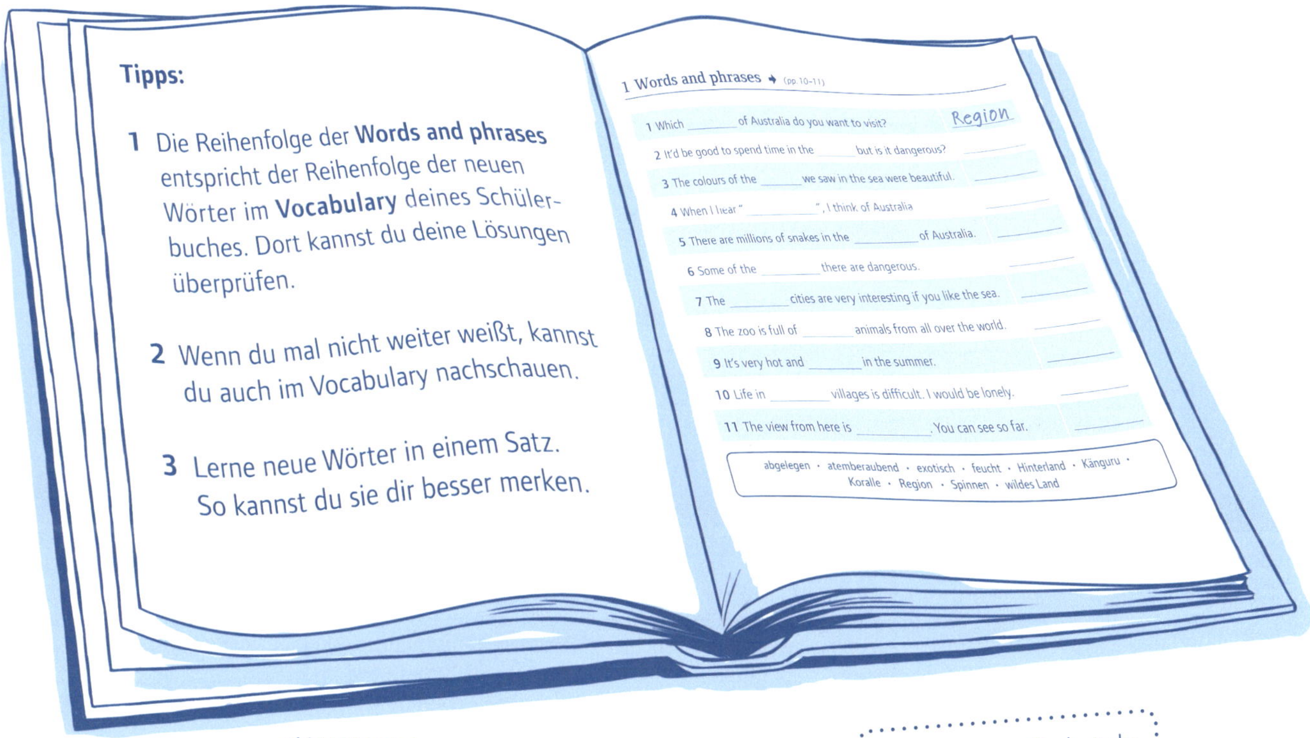

Im Anschluss an die **Words and phrases** gibt es kurze Aufgaben, Rätsel und Wortspiele, mit denen du den neuen Wortschatz weiter üben und festigen kannst.

Alle Lösungen findest du in der Mitte des Heftes.

1 Unit • Volume 5

Australia

1 Words and phrases ➜ (pp. 10–11)

1 Which region of Australia do you want to visit? The coast? The centre?	Region
2 It'd be good to spend time in the ______ but is it dangerous?	wildes Land
3 The colours of the ______ we saw in the sea were beautiful.	______
4 When I hear "______", I think of Australia.	______
5 There are millions of snakes in the ______ of Australia.	______
6 Some of the ______ there are dangerous.	______
7 The ______ cities are very interesting if you like the sea.	______
8 The zoo is full of ______ animals from all over the world.	______
9 It's very hot and ______ in the summer.	______
10 Life in ______ villages is difficult. I would be lonely.	______
11 The view from here is ______. You can see so far.	______
12 It rains a lot in ______ regions.	______
13 In the ______ it is always very green.	______
14 There are more jobs in cities and other ______ areas.	______

abgelegen • atemberaubend • exotisch • feucht • Hinterland • Känguru • Koralle • Region • Spinnen • städtisch • Tropen • tropisch • wildes Land

2 The right words

Choose the correct words from the words and phrases above to complete these sentences.

1 These are photos of the ______ storm that we were caught in. Look, they're ______.

2 It's very hot and ______ in the ______. It can make life difficult.

3 For you, ______ might be ______, but for me they are normal. I see them everyday!

4 These people live in a ______ village in the Australian ______, hundreds of miles from the nearest town.

5 You can find dangerous ______ in ______ areas in Australia, even Sydney and Canberra.

3 Words and phrases ➜ *(pp. 10–12)*

1 The ______ culture of Australia is 50,000 years old. ______

2 Would you like to ride a ______? Would it be scary? ______

3 The first white people here were ______ from England. ______

4 ______ live in trees. They're not dangerous. ______

5 Some of the spiders are ______, however. ______

6 There are 20 ______ students from France at our school. ______

7 I hope you had a nice ______ from New York. ______

8 There's a lot to see and do here. It's a ______ town. ______

9 The ______ attractions are in the centre. They're really old. ______

10 The oldest ______ is 300 years old. ______

11 White people ______ here over 200 years ago. ______

12 This is now the ______ area of the town. It's very popular. ______

13 The ______ ______ with the banks is in the city centre. ______

Aborigine • angesagteste • Austausch- • Flug • Geschäftsviertel • giftig • historisch • Kamel • Koalas • lebendig • sich niederlassen • Stadtviertel • Sträflinge

4 Match the parts

Match the two parts of the dialogues.

1 So the convicts were the first people here?
2 Do you live here?
3 So, are you a student?
4 How was your flight?
5 Are there a lot of historical attractions here?
6 What's that noise? Was that a koala?
7 Is this the business district?
8 I like this quarter. It's lively.
9 Have you been in the bush?
10 I like everything about Australia.

a No, I'm an exchange student.
b Yes, and trendy too.
c No, that was the Aboriginals.
d No, stupid! It was a camel!
e No, I've got my own business.
f No, not yet. I'd like to go, though.
g Yes, this was the first quarter that was settled.
h What, even the spiders?
i No, that's miles away.
j It was interesting to see the region from above.

5 Words and phrases ➜ (p. 12)

1 That is not a bat, it's a ________ _____. But they very similar.	________
2 Urban ________ are found everywhere in Europe.	________
3 I don't know much about the ________ *Carmen*.	________
4 I walked along the _______ and watched the boats.	________
5 My house is a _____________ ride from here. It's not far.	________
6 We had a _____________ holiday there last August.	________
7 My favourite café is on the ______________ by the sea.	________
8 A student _________ us through the museum and knew so much.	________
9 It's important to be _________ and always tell the truth.	________
10 He asked for my _______ on his idea. I told him I liked it.	________
11 ________ a bus from here into the centre. It's a ten-minute ride.	________

ehrlich • Flughund • Fuchs • führen • Hafenviertel • halbstündig • Kai • Meinung • nehmen • Oper • zweiwöchig

6 Wrong!

Circle the mistake(s) in each line and write the correct word(s) on the right.
Two sentences are correct – which?

1 It's a ten-hours train journey to the remottest part of the region. ________
2 We found a nice and trend restaurant in the student quater. ________
3 The British sent their convincts to Australia. ________
4 When visiting coasted areas, don't take corral from the sea. ________
5 I knew there were koalas and kangeroos here, but not kamels. ________
6 Quite a few exotisch animals in Australia are poisenous ________
7 We love the waterfront, the quays in particular. ________
8 You find postcards of the Oper House everywhere. ________
9 My dad's buiseness is guiding tours to the historical atractions. ________
10 I had never heard about flying foxes before today. ________
11 To be honnest, I never knew flying foxes lived in urbain areas. ________
12 The outback is very important in aboriginal culture. ________

7 Words and phrases ➜ *(pp. 12–13)*

1 The coastal road is very ______. It's one of the most beautiful roads I've seen. ______

2 The whole area was ______ in 2010. It looks so different now. ______

3 The Opera House is the ______ of Sydney. It's very famous. ______

4 The beach here is a swimmer's ______. It's fantastic. ______

5 We watched the boats in the ______, then we went swimming in the sea. ______

6 ______ ______ in 1975 there was no Internet. What did people do? ______

7 I'm not British. I'm an ______. I'm from Sydney. ______

8 My host family ______ very kind when I was in Australia. ______

9 I like rugby, ______ I don't play it well. ______

10 Let's have a ______ on Sunday. Come to our garden at 3 pm. ______

11 To learn to surf you need a ______ and some good waves. ______

12 My mouth is dry. I can't ______. ______

13 They're really rich. They've got ______ of money. ______

14 They send their children to a very expensive ______ school. ______

Australier • Bucht • damals • Grillfest • obwohl • Paradies • privat • schlucken • schön • Surfbrett • Tonne • verwandeln • Wahrzeichen • war

8 Fitting everything together

In each line, (circle) a word that doesn't fit. Then replace this with a word that you have circled in another line.

1 Quentin isn't at the local school. He goes to a (stunning) school. p______

2 The area will look different soon. They have plans to catch it. ______

3 That's not just an old building. It's a famous local paradise. ______

4 The scenery here is more than beautiful. It's really private. ______

5 The beaches here are a surfer's board. They are just fantastic. ______

6 I spent more time in the water than on my landmark when I first learned to surf. ______

7 I love the summer. It's always great weather for tons. ______

8 The beach was empty this morning, but now there are barbecues of people. ______

9 Later we can swallow a bus and watch a film, if you like. ______

10 My mouth is so dry I'm finding it hard to transform anything. ______

9 Words and phrases ➜ *(pp. 13–14)*

1 They welcomed me and ____________ me into their group very quickly. ____________

2 He doesn't say much. He's not very ____________. ____________

3 Do you have ____________ as a school subject? ____________

4 I was worried at first but ___ ___ ___ everything was OK. ____________

5 I _____ a bit ____________ when I got to Australia. ____________

6 What do you do on ____________ _____? Open presents? ____________

7 Travelling alone made me ____________. ____________

8 Are Germans as ____________ as Aussies? ____________

9 I saw her on the _____ _____ day of my holiday. ____________

10 It's hot. Don't forget your ____________. ____________

allererster • am Ende • annehmen • Fotografie • gesprächig • Heiligabend • Heimweh haben • locker • selbstbewusst • Sonnenschutzmittel

10 Three into one

Join the three parts (one from each column) to make sentences.

1 I think it's good to be	a self-confident	I is to learn to do things yourself.
2 It's natural to feel	b talkative	II route is definitely more interesting.
3 The best way to become	c trendy	III because it's where the students live.
4 My dad's quite	d accepted	IV the first time you're away on your own.
5 It's a bit longer, but the	e easy-going	V until I joined a team at school.
6 This area is quite	f scenic	VI and not worry about things too much.
7 We went to a	g a bit homesick	VII but I am happier to listen.
8 I didn't really feel fully	h lively at night	VIII new place last night. It was fun.

11 Quick quiz

1 What's the abbreviation for a barbecue? ____________

2 What's the short name for someone from Australia? ____________

3 What's the name given to December 24th? ____________

4 What do people put on to stop being burned in hot weather? ____________

5 What is the art of taking pictures with a camera? ____________

12 Words and phrases ➜ *(pp. 15–17)*

1 Aussies often say "___ ______". It shows they are relaxed.	______
2 He often plays with his ______ after school.	______
3 ______ texts present ______.	______
4 I find ______ ______ hard.	______
5 He ______ that we should all learn Chinese. I don't think he's right.	______
6 She asked us to ______ but we couldn't think of anything good.	______
7 Some people ______ these plans but many more like them.	______
8 I'm not just ______ my opinion. It's a fact.	______
9 He goes ______ for his holidays. It's sunnier there, he says.	______
10 ___ ______ ___ the weather, it's also fun.	______
11 ______, I would prefer to stay at home.	______
12 Can we talk? I'd like to ______ something private with you.	______

argumentativ • Argument • behaupten • besprechen • Erörterungen • gegen etwas sein • ins Ausland • Kein Problem • Kumpel • persönlich • so viele Ideen wie möglich sammeln • außer • äußern

13 Almost the same

Match the sentences with similar meanings.

1 No worries, mate.
2 He gave us his take on the situation.
3 He opposed what we suggested.
4 You could argue that, I suppose.
5 We could brainstorm a few ideas.
6 We generally have foreign holidays.
7 I'm just saying what I think.
8 We have a few things to discuss.
9 Life was very different back then.
10 Personally, I think it's a bad idea.

a That's one way of supporting your point.
b Let's see if we can think of anything.
c I'm stating my opinion.
d This is something we need to talk about.
e He told us his opinion.
f Things have changed a lot since.
g Most years we go abroad in summer.
h That's fine, really.
i We shouldn't do it, if you ask me.
j He was really against it.

14 Words and phrases ➔ (p. 17)

1 Sport is fun. ________, it's healthy. ________

2 Everyone should do some sport, ___ ___ ___. ________

3 ___ ___ ___ ___, it's good for teamwork. ________

4 ___ ___ ___ ___, you can injure yourself. ________

5 But some people ___ ___ ___ ___. ________

6 Being tall is an ________ in some sports. ________

7 But being short is not always a ________. ________

8 Dad often ___ ________ between us. He says I'm not as good. ________

9 ___ ___ ___, I'll describe the problem. ________

10 ________, we need to have a party. ________

11 ________, we should discuss who to invite. ________

12 ________, we should decide who will pay for it? ________

anderer Ansicht sein • andererseits • außerdem • drittens • einerseits • erstens • meiner Meinung nach • Nachteil • Vergleiche anstellen • Vorteil • zunächst • zweitens

15 Fill the gaps

Use one word from each of two boxes to complete the sentences.

addition • take • the • back • to

in • other • different • settled • then

to • view • hand • tropics • in • with

1 It's cold out, and in ________ ________ that, I'm tired.

2 Everyone should learn a foreign language, ________ my ________.

3 Foreign holidays are expensive, true. But on the ________ ________, they teach you about the world.

4 Some people say we shouldn't kill any animals. Many others ________ a different ________.

5 It's never really cold in ________ ________, which is one of the things I like about life there.

6 Australia was not empty before white people ________ ________ the country.

7 My grandparents came here in the 1930s. ________ ________ the population was quite small.

8 ________ start ________, I'm going to show you a short film of my trip.

16 Words and phrases ➜ *(pp. 18–19)*

1 The ship hit a ______ in front of the harbour. ______

2 The road was ______ after a week of rain. ______

3 I'm ______ ______ be better this year. ______

4 The garden is full of ants and other ______. ______

5 We found a snake in the garden, perhaps a ______. ______

6 ______, it didn't see us. ______

7 I ______ dogs ______ ______. ______

8 Snakes are ______ easy-going. ______

9 – But they are dangerous if you ______ them. ______

10 You can't be ______ by ______. ______

11 There are lots of ______ in Australia and Africa. ______

12 – Yes, you don't want to ______ ______ them! ______

13 I ______ along the reef yesterday. ______

fest entschlossen • glücklicherweise • hauptsächlich • Insekt • Krokodil • Mensch • Nachtfalter • provozieren • Python • Riff • schnorcheln • überflutet • verletzen • vorziehen • zufällig begegnen

17 Talking about presentations

Match the two parts to make sentences.

1 We talked about going to see the film but
2 You'll never guess who I bumped
3 Before you start writing an essay, it's useful
4 Unless you have been abroad, it's difficult
5 They showed us where we could catch a bus
6 We spent the morning on a boat
7 I'm so busy these days. I've got tons
8 My sister knows what she wants. She's determined
9 I'm quite an active person. I prefer doing things
10 Good argumentative texts should outline both arguments

a to brainstorm some ideas first.
b to begin with.
c to the best beach in the area.
d of work to do for school.
e in the end we decided to stay at home.
f to staying at home watching TV.
g to make comparisons between countries.
h into when I was in town yesterday.
i to be a professional musician later on.
j in the bay. It was fantastic.

18 Words and phrases ➔ (pp. 20–22)

1 We grow vegetables in the ______ in the garden.	______
2 At night you see lights of the ______ and the boats.	______
3 His escape was very exciting and ______.	______
4 The hotel is tiny but the ______ ______ great.	______
5 In summer this beach is ______, too many people.	______
6 ______ schools are often very small. Schools in the city are bigger.	______
7 ______ houses often look boring. I like houses in the city centre more.	______
8 Australia is a ______ country, as big as Europe.	______
9 Rivers make it possible to have ______ harbours.	______
10 The winters are quite ______ here. It's never very cold.	______
11 Skiing is popular in ______ areas.	______
12 My parents are very ______ and not at all modern.	______
13 The city is ______, so it's fun to cycle.	______
14 He wrote a ______ text about Grandma and used lots of adjectives.	______
15 ______ help you sound better when you write.	______

altmodisch • auf dem Land • Ausstattung • bergig • beschreibend • Binnen- • dramatisch • flach • Gewächshaus • Kollokation • Küstenlinie • mild • riesig • überfüllt • Vorstadt-

19 Keywords

Rewrite the sentences using the keywords so they mean the same as the original. Don't change the keyword in any way.

1 The shop stays open day and night.	hour	That's ______
2 What do you think about the plan?	take	What's ______
3 If you ask me, it's a great idea.	view	It's a ______
4 I've never been abroad before.	very	This is ______
5 I'll do everything I can to win.	determined	I am ______
6 Dan says spiders are cool. I disagree.	different	I ______

20 Words and phrases → (pp. 23–26)

1 I ________ with you. I think you're wrong.	________
2 What he said was ______ and ________. That's why I cried.	________
3 You're talking ________! You are wrong again.	________
4 They ______ a car, but not the same opinions.	________
5 You say Australia is great? I ________ agree, I love it!	________
6 ____ ______ I can't agree with you.	________
7 You ______ __ ______ there. Yes, perhaps that's right.	________
8 I'll maybe give her a _____ ________. I don't know her very well.	________
9 My parents can ski. ___ ____ I.	________
10 I like dogs. ___ _____ my brother.	________
12 I'd love to be rich. ___ ______ my friend.	________

auch (3x) • dummes Zeug • Geschenkgutschein • leider • nicht ganz Unrecht haben • nicht übereinstimmen • sich teilen • total • unhöflich • verletzend

21 Scrambled report

Put the parts in the correct order. The first one has been done for you.

a Australia is a vast country, but it has a relatively small population,

b course crocodiles. Almost every week there's a dramatic

h story in the news about someone bumping into a "saltie" but

d being easy-going. Perhaps that's an advantage when you share

f coastline, and that's mainly what makes it a surfer's

e so it certainly isn't overcrowded. Of course, millions of

c but it's a different story in rural areas and particularly in

g people live in suburban areas of cities like Sydney and Melbourne,

i paradise. Aussies are famous for their love of sports and for

j the Outback. As Australia is an island, it has a very long

l the country with so many exotic and dangerous animals, like

m luckily not many people are seriously injured by them.

k poisonous snakes and spiders, and huge pythons, and of

Answer: a ☐ ☐ ☐ ☐ ☐ ☐ ☐ ☐ ☐ ☐ ☐ ☐

22 Words and phrases ➔ (pp. 26–27)

1 What ______ ____ music do you like best? Rock, pop, rap?	______
2 I watched a game of ______ on TV. It was a Major League game.	______
3 Dad is outside. He ___ ______ in the garden.	______
4 If I had the ______, I'd choose to live abroad.	______
5 There's a ______ of rain tomorrow.	______
6 I did some ______ ______ last year at a business called Cornelsen.	______
7 My mother is a doctor. She works in the local ______.	______
8 She says her ______ are all very patient.	______
9 Parliament ______ the future of the EU.	______
10 We still have a problem with ______.	______
11 I heard someone say something ______ to a man from India.	______
12 Grandma used to be a ______ actor and was very rich.	______

Art • Chance • Fußball • graben • Klinik • Möglichkeit • Patient • Praktikum • professionell • Rassismus • rassistisch • über etwas debattieren

23 Missing!

Add missing words to **two** of the four gaps to complete the sentences.

1 My family ______ love most ______ sorts ______ professional sport, ______ be honest, except soccer, which we find boring.

2 I had the ______ possibility ______ doing work ______ experience after ______ school, which was great.

3 I think ______ people ______ say things like that are racist, and ______ does the law, in ______ fact.

4 I'm ______ afraid I don't agree ______ you on that, but ______ your sister has ______ point, in my view.

5 It's just ______ nonsense that ______ disagreeing ______ someone means you ______ being hurtful.

6 It might ______ look like ______ old-fashioned hotel, but the facilities it has ______ fantastic ______.

7 We debate ______ lots of topics at school, such ______ whether doctors should always ______ tell patients ______ clinics bad news.

8 Personally, I ______ would prefer a gift voucher ______ a present I didn't really ______ want, and so ______ my friends.

24 Words and phrases ➜ (p. 27)

1 There are sometimes ducks and ________ on this river. ________________

2 The winners of the competition got a golden ________. ________________

3 Do you have an ________ for "Best Teacher" at your school? ________________

4 She loved animals and always ________ ____ _____ animal rights. ________________

5 She got an award in ______________ of her work and was very proud. ________________

6 We must make a ________ __________ racism. Then it might stop. ________________

7 Who _____ _________ sportsperson of the year? ________________

8 He was ____________ _____ his reaction because it seemed unfair. ________________

9 Toni and Felix are brothers but play for ____________ teams. ________________

10 We saw lots of funny monkeys and ______ in the zoo. ________________

11 You have the best view from the front _____. You're nearer the stage. ________________

12 I was very ________ because of what he said. I cried. ________________

Anerkennung • Auszeichnung • ernannt werden • gegnerisch • gekränkt • Haltung gegenüber • kritisieren • Medaille • Menschenaffe • Reihe • Schwan • sich einsetzen

25 More about Sydney

Complete the text with words from the box.

Aboriginal • abroad • addition • attraction • business • capital • convicts • events • foreign • human • landmarks • natural • population • settled • tools • transformed • waterfront

The first people who lived in the area we know as Sydney probably came from northern Australia. **1** _________ stone **2** _________ have been discovered that show evidence of **3** _________ activity in the area since about 50,000 years ago. Sydney is the **4** _________ of New South Wales – but not of the country – and surrounds the world's largest **5** _________ harbour, which is why the **6** _________ is the main **7** _________ of the city. The first Europeans who **8** _________ there were the British. However, the city has **9** _________ from a destination for **10** _________ into a major international centre. It has a **11** _________ of around 4.5 million, and 1.5 million of these were born **12** _________: more than 250 different languages are spoken in Sydney. Sydney is also open for **13** _________. It is home to many **14** _________ banks, and has hosted **15** _________ such as the 2000 summer Olympics. In **16** _________, millions of tourists visit the city each year to see the famous **17** _________.

26 Words and phrases ➜ *(pp. 27–29)*

1 How did the team celebrate their ___________? Were they very happy?	___________
2 I didn't hear the player's ___________. What did he say?	___________
3 She didn't do it. She's ___________.	___________
4 It isn't fair! You _____ the _____ _____ me _____ everything!	___________
5 ___________ we can't come to your party.	___________
6 Dad was ___________ as a child. It was horrible, he says.	___________
7 Their ___________ shows they're brothers. They look so similar.	___________
8 My uncle works in the coal ___________.	___________
9 I always enjoy her ___________. She makes me laugh.	___________
10 The police are investigating the ___________.	___________
11 The fans ___________ the other team.	___________
12 My first book was a big ___________ for me.	___________
13 *Doctor Who* is a very old TV ___________ from the UK.	___________
14 The book is really good. Its ___________ is London 100 years ago.	___________

ausbuhen • Aussehen • Bemerkung • Errungenschaft • Gesellschaft • Industrie • jm. die Schuld geben • leider • mobben • Schauplatz • Serie • Sieg • unschuldig • Vorfall

27 The right word

Circle the correct word to complete the sentences.

1 She's wearing the winner's **award** • **achievement** • **medal** she got in the Olympics.

2 It's normal, but I disagree with fans who boo the **opposed** • **opposing** • **opposite** team.

3 If you sit in the front **line** • **row** • **rank** you get a fantastic view of the game.

4 **I'm afraid of** • **Luckily** • **Unfortunately** bullying is still a problem in many schools.

5 It's important to **stand up for** • **debate** • **be determined for** what you believe is right.

6 Everyone should **take a stand against** • **put the blame on** • **criticize** racism.

7 We had a very **live** • **lively** • **living** lesson when we debated problems in society.

8 I'm not against soccer players' high salaries; others **take** • **make** • **find** a different view.

9 He made a **hurtful** • **talkative** • **descriptive** comment that really upset me.

10 People in rural areas say cities are **overcrowdy** • **overcrowding** • **overcrowded** .

28 Crossword

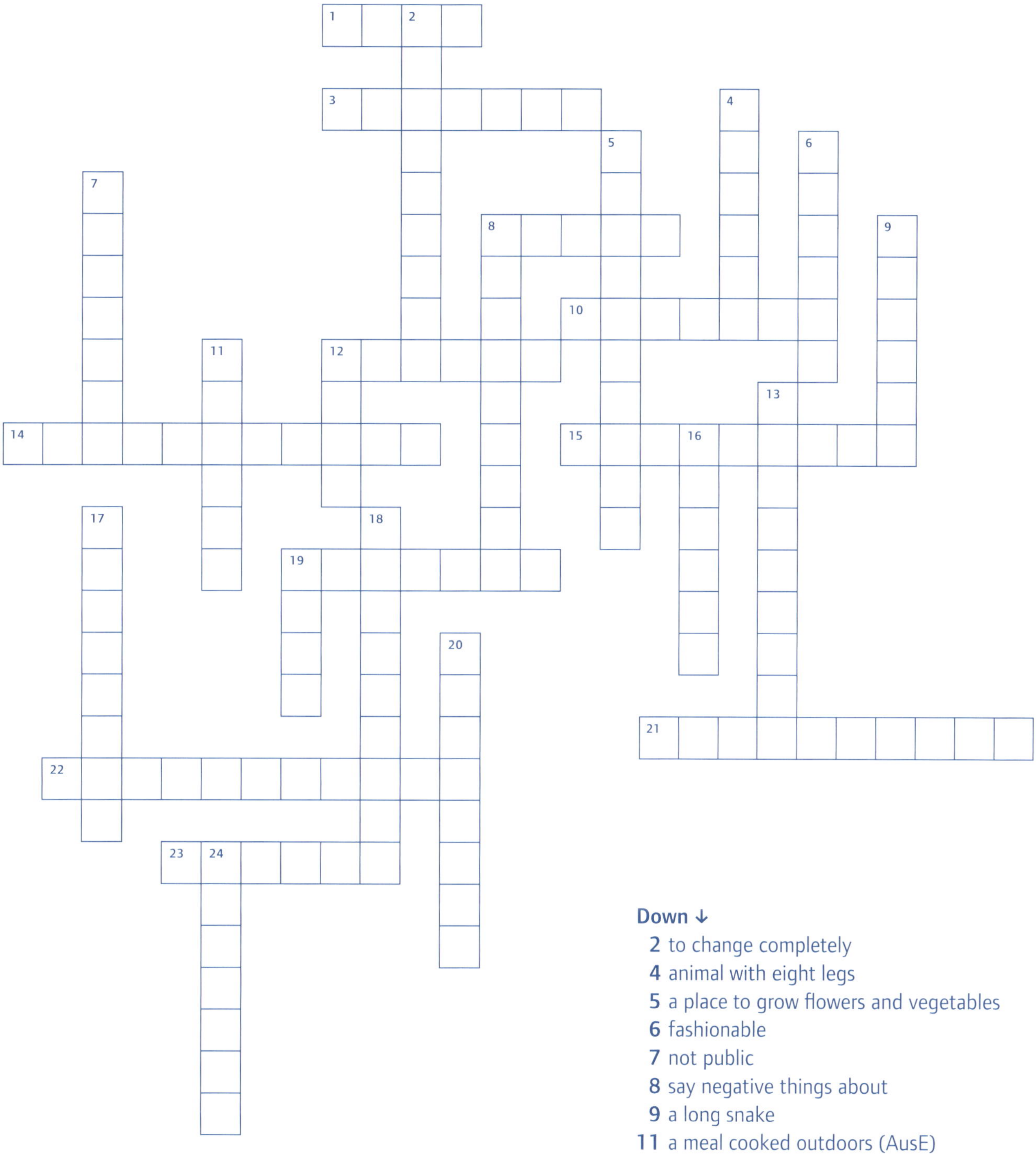

Across →

1 friend
3 area of a city
8 desert animal
10 badly hurt
12 far away
14 with too many people
15 used to stop burning
19 breathe in the sea
21 the way sb./sth. looks
22 words that go together to make a useful expression
23 to be against something

Down ↓

2 to change completely
4 animal with eight legs
5 a place to grow flowers and vegetables
6 fashionable
7 not public
8 say negative things about
9 a long snake
11 a meal cooked outdoors (AusE)
12 not polite
13 dangerous animal in rivers and the sea
16 football
17 animal that jumps a lot
18 where the sea meets the land
19 big white bird
20 very beautiful
24 someone a doctor helps

Relationships

1 Words and phrases ➔ (pp. 34–36)

1 Dad is a very good ________ and takes super photos. ________

2 I'm trying to read a ________ by Charles Dickens – in English. ________

3 I ________ I know all the people in my village, except the new ones. ________

4 He must come. He made me a ________ and said he would. ________

5 After the swim, my lips were ________ from the sea water. ________

6 An Indian doctor ________ her after her accident. ________

7 My hair's too long. Tomorrow I'm going to get a new ________. ________

8 OK, eat my chips. ________ ________ ________ ________. I don't really want them. ________

9 ________ your parents ________ in the last ________ for the Bundestag? ________

10 His favourite ________ is ________. He's very interested in the news. ________

11 Don't say anything about his nose. He's very ________ about it. ________

12 Money is a big problem for many people. Is it an ________ in your family? ________

13 ________ we were in the car, I immediately remembered my phone. ________

14 Are all computer games a ________ of time, or can you learn something too? ________

behandeln • empfindlich • Fotograf • Haarschnitt • Politik • Roman • salzig • schätzen • sobald • Streitfrage • Thema • Verschwendung • Versprechen • Von mir aus gern • Wahlen • wählen

2 The right words

elections • fine • haircut • novel • once • politics • promise • reckon • sensitive • subject • treat • vote • waste

Choose the correct words from the box to complete these sentences.

1 I ________ you can have my ________ ________ I have finished it.

2 Don't talk about ________. It's such a boring ________.

3 It's time for a me to get a ________, I ________.

4 If you don't to ________, that's ________ by me.

5 I watched a terrible programme about the recent ________. It was a ________ of time.

6 People can be ________, so you should ________ everyone with kindness.

3 Words and phrases ➜ *(p. 37)*

1 I didn't see the ______ ________ in the park because it was so dark. ____________

2 I fell on my face and hurt my ______. And I ______ my jeans. ____________

3 The ______ on my phone are too small for my big fingers. ____________

4 I was very nervous. My hands ________ so badly that I dropped my cup. ____________

5 Everyone should learn ________ _____. It can help you if there's an accident. ____________

6 Nobody can __________ under water naturally. ____________

7 The ______ on his hands was very hard. ____________

8 After the race her _________ were very red. She looked like a tomato. ____________

9 Your _______ is the number of times per minute your hearts beats. ____________

10 The _______ in your head needs _________ to work. ____________

11 Their village is very __________ from other towns. ____________

12 The boat started to ______ in the storm. ____________

13 John is very clever, probably the most ______________ boy in our class. ____________

14 We ________________ go out for a nice meal, perhaps once a month. ____________

ab und zu • atmen • Baumstamm • entfernt • Erste Hilfe • Gehirn • Haut • intelligent • Kinn • Puls • Sauerstoff • sinken • Taste • Wange • zerreißen • zittern

4 Logic!

Match the two parts logically.

1 The message contained some spelling mistakes.
2 I wouldn't say she's a friend of mine.
3 I don't think there is much sugar in this.
4 I don't like swimming very much.
5 The photo is not very clear at all.
6 I'm sure I'm not dead.
7 I just can't think of the answer.
8 I wanted to say something intelligent.
9 I don't think he's a farmer, you know.
10 You shouldn't stare at people.

a To be honest, I sink.
b My hands were shaking at the time.
c It's rude. How would you like it?
d However, I couldn't think of anything.
e I think his skin is too soft for that
f We just meet occasionally.
g My brain's not working today.
h I hit the wrong key a few times.
i In fact it tastes very salty.
j But I can't find my pulse.

5 Words and phrases ➔ *(pp. 37–38)*

1 She has a __________ expression, as if she's thinking about something else. __________

2 We saw pictures of __________ who came to Europe in the 1960s. __________

3 I don't know if I'll go to __________. I'd like to earn money when I'm 18. __________

4 I feel dirty! I need to buy some ______ and __________. __________

5 I need a new __________ for my teeth too. __________

6 My grandpa doesn't use __________ to clean his teeth. He uses soap! __________

7 Don't use the ________ for ______ of tomatoes. Use the cupboard instead. __________

8 It was ________ cold, about 10°, but we swam ________. We're hard! __________

9 I'm not __________ with this area: can you tell me if there is a museum here? __________

10 There was an __________ silence. I felt silly. __________

11 What's happening in the house ______ ______? Are the neighbours fighting? __________

Deodorant • Dosen • Einwanderer • Kühlschrank • nebenan • Seife • trotzdem • unangenehm • Universität • verträumt • vertraut • Zahnbürste • Zahnpasta • ziemlich

6 Missing!

Complete the words with the missing letters.

1 I like the smell of your _ _ _ **d o** _ _ _ _.

2 Do you have to pay to go to _ _ _ **v e** _ _ _ _ _ _ in Australia?

3 I felt very _ _ **k w** _ _ _ when they started arguing in front of me.

4 Don't talk about exams. It's a _ _ _ _ _ **i t** _ _ _ subject with him.

5 Can I borrow some _ _ _ _ _ **h p** _ _ _ _? I forgot mine.

6 Most nights I stay in, but _ _ _ _ _ **s i** _ _ _ _ _ _ _ I go to the cinema with friends.

7 Some people think there are too many _ _ _ _ _ **g r** _ _ _ _ _ in the country.

8 It was difficult to _ _ _ _ **a t** _ _ because of the smoke.

9 It's always nice to see a _ _ _ _ _ **l i** _ _ face when you are in a new place.

10 Is it true that plants produce _ _ _ **g e** _?

7 Words and phrases ➜ (pp. 39–42)

1 You want __________? Do more sport to get stronger. __________

2 It was too dark to see the __________ of my watch. __________

3 I __________ to tell you the news before, but I forgot. __________

4 I'm nervous __________ ____ the test tomorrow. __________

5 This is a __________ problem. It won't be easy. __________

6 I like ______-__________ __________, where the character speaks to you. __________

7 Can I make a __________? Please could you help me tomorrow morning? __________

8 The way they spoke was very __________ and difficult to understand. __________

9 Moths are __________ ____ lamps. They love them, and I don't know why. __________

10 He ______ ____ ______ with Anna as soon as he started to ______ her. __________

11 Did you know Max ____ __________ Kate again? I think they love each other. __________

12 – I thought they had __________ ____. – Yes, but only for a week. __________

13 I ______ ____ ______ Bill in 2010. I had never met him before that. __________

14 I'm a bit __________ ______ you, to be honest. You hurt me a lot. __________

Bitte • die Absicht haben • ernst • Ich-Erzählung • kennenlernen • mit jm. gehen • mit jm. zusammen sein • Muskeln • sich hingezogen fühlen • sich trennen • sich verlieben • umgangssprachlich • verärgert • über • wegen • Zeiger

8 That's wrong!

Circle the mistake(s) in each line and write the correct word(s) on the right. One line is correct – which?

1 He made a promiss not to talk about it as it's a sensative issue. __________

2 I don't spend any time argueing about politics. It's a waist of time. __________

3 He was very annoyed when I used his toothepaste. __________

4 Sorry, I ment to phone you but I just forget. __________

5 My brother is learning about first-person naratives at uniwersity. __________

6 Ocasionally he can say something inteligent, you know. __________

7 The mussels in your body need oxigene to work properly. __________

8 They made a serious request to have an informal meeting. __________

9 He was starring at the wall with a dreemy expression on his face. __________

10 My hands were shacking when I started my first haarcut. __________

9 Words and phrases ➜ (p. 42)

1 Dad still looked ____________, as if he didn't understand what I had said.	____________
2 I'm not just annoyed with her – I'm really _______ _______ her.	____________
3 It's safe. You don't need to be ____________.	____________
4 The dog looked at us with ____________ eyes. He wanted the sausage so much.	____________
5 ____________ the rain will stop soon.	____________
6 Don't be so ____________ about everything. Life is wonderful!	____________
7 I'm really ____________ with the results. I hadn't expected to do so well.	____________
8 If you tell him, he'll be _______ _______ you: really, really cross.	____________
9 He was ____________ when Jane left him and he cried for a week.	____________
10 Aunt Elvira isn't just scared of spiders. She ___ ________ ___ them.	____________

erfreut • hoffentlich • hoffnungsvoll • pessimistisch • sauer auf • schreckliche Angst vor etwas haben • todunglücklich • verängstigt • verwirrt • wütend auf

10 Three into one

Join the three parts (one from each column) to make sentences.

1 They met a few times, then	a seeing each other	I in love almost immediately.
2 I thought he might be cross, but he	b attracted	II Jim until we played football together.
3 I'm really pleased they are	c terrified	III to her, to be honest.
4 He was really confused by what	d voted	IV for making that silly mistake.
5 I used to be really	e annoyed with myself	V dating but have now broken up.
6 I didn't mean to	f happened	VI as I'm actually quite hopeful.
7 I didn't really get to	g wasn't,	VII because they are a lovely couple.
8 They met and	h sound pessimistic,	VIII of flying, but I'm much better now.
9 I found it difficult to	i know	IX he was absolutely furious.
10 He asked me how I	j started	X in the last elections.
11 I like her, but I'm not	k fell	XI because he didn't understand.
12 When I realized, I was very	l breathe	XII because of the thick smoke.

11 Words and phrases ➜ *(pp. 42–43)*

1 She was __________ when he invited her to dinner, and said "thank you". __________

2 The house was __________ empty. There was nothing at all in it. __________

3 Now Tony is divorced. He doesn't talk to his ____-wife any more. __________

4 These plants are special, because they are both ______ and ________. __________

5 He's only an ______________, not a real friend. __________

6 Please ________ your name and address on the form. __________

7 Help, I've forgotten my __________. I can't check my emails. __________

8 I __________ my ________ on social media every day. __________

9 He has an __________ with a bank in Switzerland. __________

absolut • aktualisieren • begeistert • Bekannter • eintragen • Ex- • Konto • männlich • Passwort • Status • weiblich

12 Almost the same

Match the sentences with similar meanings.

1 She had a bad time when they broke up.
2 She's been seeing him for a while.
3 She used to be his girlfriend.
4 That's the bank she uses.
5 I know her a little, but we're not friends.
6 The news was brilliant.
7 She always expects things to go wrong.
8 She doesn't understand what you mean.
9 She really wasn't very happy.
10 She was really angry.
11 She'll be really pleased with that.
12 She entered all her details.

a She was thrilled.
b She's his ex.
c She was absolutely furious.
d She has an account with them.
e She's a bit confused.
f She was quite cross.
g She completed the form.
h She's an acquaintance.
i She's dating him.
j She was heartbroken.
k She's such a pessimist.
l She'll like that, I'm sure.

13 Words and phrases ➜ (pp. 44–46)

1 There was a __________ in London yesterday: an old woman was shot.	______________________
2 The US __________ independence from Britain in 1776.	______________________
3 Jim and Gemma are __________ and ______. Their wedding was last week.	______________________
4 The doctor said Dad ________ ____ stop smoking if he wants grandchildren.	______________________
5 Fruit is important for my ______. I eat a lot of it.	______________________
6 I mustn't eat chocolate or sweets – I'm on a ______.	______________________
7 There's a lot of __________ in meat, milk, eggs and fish.	______________________
8 You need to eat well to stay __________.	______________________
9 The work is __________ ____ finish tomorrow. That's what I was told.	______________________
10 They eat a lot of ________ and pizza in Italy, don't they?	______________________
11 Let's do something __________ tonight, maybe a concert or the theatre.	______________________
12 I had ____________________ problems in Spain because I don't speak Spanish.	______________________

Diät • Ehefrau • Ehemann • Eiweiß • erklären • Ernährungsweise • gesund • Kommunikation • kulturell • Mord • Nudeln • soll • sollte

14 Quiz time!

1 Where do you keep food fresh in the kitchen?

____

2 What's the fourth word: brother: sister; wife:…

____

3 You can clean yourself with this.

____

4 You keep your money in this in a bank.

____

5 The opposite of male.

____

6 A food, like pizza, that is popular in Italy.

____

7 The opposite of formal.

____

8 A type of book that people read for pleasure.

____

9 The main part of a tree that supports the branches.

____

10 The act of killing a person illegally.

____

11 The part of your face below your mouth.

____

12 You need this to protect your online accounts.

____

15 Words and phrases ➜ (p. 47)

1 There are different sorts of ____________ to explain information in numbers. ____________

2 ____ ________ compare different numbers, perhaps over time. ____________

3 ____ ________ show parts of a whole thing. ____________

4 I don't understand this ________. What is it supposed to explain? ____________

5 The __________ person sleeps 8 hours a night. ____________

6 The official ________ of a marathon is 26.2 miles or 42.195 km. ____________

7 Is it ________ to know when you will die? I don't want to know. ____________

8 What ______________ of Germans have no jobs? ____________

9 Should children do ________ to help their parents and earn money? ____________

10 When I saw her face, I suddenly __________ that she was very unhappy. ____________

11 Grandma is sweet: she always ________ ____ us eating more than we can. ____________

auf etwas bestehen • Balkendiagramme • Durchschnitt • erkennen • Hausarbeit • Länge • nützlich • Prozentsatz • Schaubild • Statistik • Tortendiagramme

16 One from two

Match the two parts to complete the sentences.

1 I can't go out at the weekend until I've finished
2 What worries me about the bike ride is
3 Healthy eating is very important for
4 When I meet friends, I shake hands or kiss on
5 I was thirsty so I went to the fridge and took out
6 I'm not sure about buying that watch. I don't like
7 He's never asked for anything, so I was surprised by
8 All the information you need is in
9 What worries me about living abroad is
10 The scariest scene in the film is
11 Nobody can get into my account without
12 You need public transport to get to

a the cheek.
b the request.
c the password.
d the murder.
e the pie chart.
f the chores.
g the skin.
h the hands.
i the length.
j the university.
k the can.
l the communication.

17 Words and phrases ➜ (pp. 48–49)

1 We only have a small ________ of salt left – is it enough? ________

2 Different cultures have different ________, for example on civil rights. ________

3 Is your room clean and ______? ________

4 I don't have any ______ to buy a drink – can you lend me some? ________

5 It's ________ not true that young people are lazy. ________

6 Quick! It's almost nine o'clock. We're ________ _____ _____ time. ________

7 Don't force him, just ________ him. Then ________ he'll learn. ________

8 ________ ________ like being tidy are good; others are bad. ________

9 When was the trade ________ between the USA and Cuba signed? ________

10 He gave me the chance to ________ myself fully and tell him what I thought. ________

11 I must ________ that this is your own decision, and I don't agree with it. ________

12 We have ______ at home. We love eggs! ________

13 We stopped arguing and ________ that the argument had been silly. ________

14 When I leave the office, please ________ me to go to the bank. ________

Bargeld • betonen • einfach • ermutigen • gewisse(r, s) • Gewohnheit • Henne • kein Geld mehr haben • Menge • ordentlich • erinnern • sich ausdrücken • sich einig sein • Vereinbarung • vielleicht • Wert

18 Missing!

Add missing words to **two** of the **four** gaps to complete the sentences.

1 We weren't going to reach ________ agreement ________, so we ________ had to agree ________ disagree.

2 Many ________ families insist ________ ________ kids doing ________ chores if they want pocket money.

3 If you ________ want to get ________ job and not go to ________ university, that's fine ________ me.

4 The car hit ________ tree ________ trunk, but fortunately there ________ no ________ serious damage.

5 I've been staring ________ this crossword puzzle ________ hours ________ but I just ________ can't do it.

6 I'm really ________ pleased ________ the mark I got for ________ narrative I wrote for ________ school.

7 We're a little ________ late ________ because ________ the traffic, but ________ least we have arrived.

8 I'm generally attracted ________ ________ people who have ________ positive take on ________ things.

19 Words and phrases ➔ (p. 50)

1 How many ___________ did Germany accept in 2015? ___________

2 William is 15 and plays in the ________ team of his football club. ___________

3 I work for a government ________________ that helps homeless people. ___________

4 I don't like bosses. I want to _____ my own business later. ___________

5 She wrote her first novel at 17. It was ____________ the next year. ___________

6 You always help me – thank you. Your _____________ is very important to me. ___________

7 We had to _____ ____ a ______ when we arrived at the hotel. ___________

8 The ___________ to the city is 10 miles. ___________

ausfüllen • Entfernung • Flüchtling • Formular • Freundschaft • Jugend • leiten • Organisation • veröffentlichen

20 Scrambled report

Put the parts in the correct order. The first one has been done for you.

a There are a lot of stories about immigrants and

c left behind everything they are familiar with and that they

e in or maybe even will not want to try to adapt to

d people who come from cultures which have very different

j to work and make a contribution; and we must remember that

f on TV these days: it's one of the most sensitive

g and the habits of their own country. Others disagree and

b ought to be treated with respect and given our

i values as perhaps they will find it difficult to fit

l say it is our responsibility to help these people who have

n their new society but will keep their language, religion

k issues we have today. Some people say that we should not accept

m friendship. It's important to realize that immigrants want

o many refugees travel great distances to be safe and not feel terrified every day.

h refugees published in the newspapers and shown

Answer: a

21 Words and phrases ➜ *(p. 50)*

1 He doesn't have a car, so he always travels by public ________. ________

2 When he arrived, the biggest problem ____ ________ was the language. ________

3 It's hard to _____ ____ without English: you're not part of the group. ________

4 You're 22 now. _____ like a man, not a child. ________

5 You'll soon ________ to the culture when you understand it better. ________

6 I quickly _____ ______ ____ speaking English. It only took a few weeks. ________

7 I missed the bus and ________ ____ walking. ________

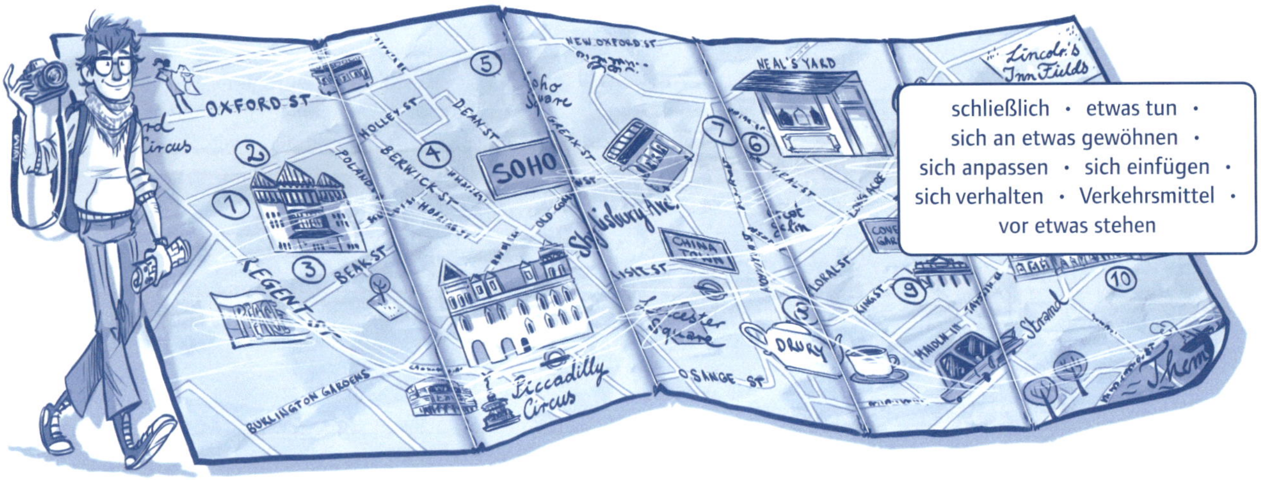

schließlich • etwas tun • sich an etwas gewöhnen • sich anpassen • sich einfügen • sich verhalten • Verkehrsmittel • vor etwas stehen

22 Keywords

Rewrite the sentences using the **keywords** so they mean the same as the original. Don't change the keyword in any way.

1 We haven't got any more eggs.	out	________
2 I didn't forget it was her birthday because he told me.	reminded	________
3 I don't eat everything because I don't want to be so fat.	on	________
4 The moon is about 400,000 km from the Earth.	between	________
5 We went for a swim in the sea although it was cold.	anyway	________
6 My parents were unhappy that my hair was too long.	length	________
7 I hated the hotel at first, but now it's not a problem.	got	________
8 After a while, we had an argument.	ended	________
9 There will be a big problem for us soon.	facing	________
10 I don't have much money.	amount	________

23 Words and phrases ➜ (p. 50)

1 You made the mistake and now you have to take ________________ for it. ________________

2 He managed to find a job ________ two weeks of arriving in Germany. ________________

3 I asked an __________ for help to find a job. ________________

4 He's not a nurse, but he works as a _______ for old people. ________________

5 A baby is totally ______________ _____its mother for the first months. ________________

6 We were very lucky in South Africa: we _____ ____ _____ a family of lions. ________________

7 We stayed at home last summer: we _________ go __________. ________________

abhängig von • Berater • die Möglichkeit bekommen, etwas zu tun • innerhalb von • nirgendwohin • Pfleger • Verantwortung

24 A conversation

Put the replies in this dialogue in the correct order.

1 What's the matter? You look upset. Are you cross about something?

2 Really? Why? You normally do well above average in all your subjects.

3 You mean the bar charts and the pie charts?

4 Well, don't worry. Perhaps you did better than you think.

5 Don't be so pessimistic. Perhaps your teacher will be pleased with your work.

6 But it's his job to encourage you. And he knows you're intelligent

7 Don't say that.

a I know, but this time I had problems with the statistics we had to do.

b Am I? It made me realize that I don't think I can go to university.

c I'm not sure about that. I didn't do everything we were supposed to do.

d I'm pretty sure he won't. He insists on nice tidy work with a good amount of detail.

e Well, I'm just annoyed with myself because of the homework. I only got a "D".

f Yes. I took too long doing my chores and then simply ran out of time.

25 Words and phrases ➔ (p. 51)

1 I didn't go inside the shop. I just looked at the ______ ________. ______________

2 Oh dear, tomato sauce on my shirt. I should wear an ______ when I cook. ______________

3 Not so fast! Why ____ you ___ such ___ ______? ______________

4 We ________ eat around 7 pm, sometimes earlier, never much later. ______________

5 My legs are ______ after that walk yesterday. ______________

6 We all played football, ________ my grandma. ______________

7 The two of us did the work in ________. ______________

8 Heathrow is an important ____ for aeroplanes between the USA and Europe. ______________

9 Everything here is ________. No machines were used. ______________

einschließlich • es eilig haben • handgemacht • Knotenpunkt • normalerweise • Schaufenster • Schürze • steif • Tandem

26 The right word

Circle the correct word to complete the sentences.

1 I'll be very **cross • crossed • crossing** with you if you are late again.

2 He's not **normalwise • normally • normal** so sensitive about things like that.

3 This tastes very **saltish • salted • salty** . Let's add some more water.

4 He was quiet, but he was nice when you got to **knowing • known • know** him.

5 My dad has two **hairscuts • haircuts • haircuttings** a month. He likes short hair.

6 I haven't changed my profile for ages. I ought to **update • redate • actual** it.

7 My friends paid for my whole holiday, **include • included • including** the flights.

8 In cities, it's common not to know the people who live **near • next • beside** door.

9 I don't think politics **is • are** boring. I find **them • it** really interesting.

10 To join the club, all you have to do is **complete • fill • write** in a form.

11 Slow down! Why are you in such **an • a • the** hurry? We've got plenty of time.

12 I think you should have more **diet • muscle • protein** in your food.

27 Dialogues

Match the two parts of these dialogues.

1 This shop is quite expensive.
2 What do you call a bike for two?
3 Has he got a job?
4 I haven't run so far for years.
5 It's difficult to understand them. They speak so fast.
6 So, are you going to start cooking?
7 You said you go to the hub twice a week.
8 Imagine what it would be like to be a pilot.
9 My first job was to do the shop windows.
10 I have to adapt to the new team. I don't know any of them.
11 What do those statistics show?
12 Did you do chores when you were younger?

a Yes, you'd get to travel a lot!
b Don't worry. You'll get used to it.
c The percentage of refugees in each city.
d Yes, on average.
e Wow! That's a big responsibility.
f Yes, everything's handmade. That's why.
g Not really. He's a carer for his parents.
h I'm sure you'll fit in well.
i Well, I was supposed to.
j A tandem, I think.
k Sure. Where's the apron?
l I know, we're going to be stiff tomorrow.

28 Missing!

Complete these sentences by writing in the missing words or parts of words.

1 It's useful to know how to do ________ aid, in case something happens to someone.
2 Winter sports like skiing are ________ on the weather: they need snow.
3 He was absolutely ________broken when he couldn't go to the Olympics.
4 I don't buy much, but I love looking in shop ________ to see what there is.
5 ________fully everything will be finished soon so we can all go home early.
6 I travel everywhere by public ________port. It's not always quick, but it's cheap.
7 My dad's an ad________. His job is to en________ people to find solutions to their own problems.
8 They have different opinions on everything and never reach ________ment on anything.
9 I'm sure I don't need to re________ you how important good work is to this ________ation.
10 School is ________mally where young people form their most important friend________.

Big dreams – small steps

1 Words and phrases ➜ *(pp. 56–57)*

1 Amy's brother was in the ______ and fought in Afghanistan. ______

2 My sister is a good ______. She can run 200 metres in 32 seconds. ______

3 Is ______ ______ maybe the biggest problem facing the Arctic today? ______

4 Bikes ______ __ ______ to pollution in cities. ______

5 My grandpa ______ clocks until he was 80. ______

6 We're doing a ______ experiment at school tomorrow. ______

7 I would like to try ______ one day. It's like flying! ______

8 You've ______ a lot this year, and I'm very proud of you. ______

9 It's important to have ______ in life, so that you know where you are going. ______

10 The ______ for your report is next Monday. You must hand it in by then. ______

11 He ______ to achieve his goal. He needed 90 points but only got 89. ______

12 I sent them my ______ yesterday. I hope I get the job! ______

13 77 people ______ ______ the job, but only one will get it. ______

Armee • Athletin • beim Versuch scheitern • Bewerbung • Erderwärmung • erreichen • etwas bewirken • Fallschirmspringen • letzter Termin • reparieren • sich um etwas bewerben • wissenschaftlich • Ziel

2 The right words

Choose the correct words from the box to complete these sentences. Not all the words are needed.

1 Some people don't accept the ______ proof for ______ ______.

2 I'm thinking about ______ to join the ______.

3 One ______ of mine is to go ______.

4 The training made a ______ for the ______.

5 I ______ a lot today. I completed that job ______.

6 I ______ to understand why you didn't take the computer to be ______.

7 The ______ for ______ is next Friday.

achieved • achieving • application • applications • applied • applying • army • athletes • deadline • difference • fail • failing • global warming • goal • goals • repaired • repairing • scientific • scientist • skydiving

3 Words and phrases ➜ (p. 58)

1 In class yesterday, we read a three-page __________ from a novel. __________

2 I'm the new ______-captain of the team, so quite important. __________

3 We live in Bonn, the __________ capital of the Federal Republic of Germany. __________

4 Hurry up! The film is ________ ____ start. __________

5 He spends hours practising his throws on the basketball ________. __________

6 Jack and Jim are twins and they look __________. __________

7 I first _________ when I was 14. I already had a little beard. __________

8 He's good but should think of the others and ______ the football more. __________

9 I don't read the _______: I don't go to church and I'm not ___________. __________

10 My dad and my uncles are all ______: none of them have any hair at all. __________

11 Can you _____ what's wrong with the picture? __________

12 I went red because it was so _________________. __________

abspielen • Auszug • ehemalig • erkennen • glatzköpfig • identisch • kurz davor • peinlich • religiös • sich rasieren • Spielfeld • Vize-

4 Match the parts

Choose the right ending to complete the sentences.

1 I remembered my umbrella just when I was about
2 He gave us all a surprise when he came to school
3 In class we spent some time discussing an extract
4 I called the teacher the wrong name in class. It was
5 They were on the court practising how
6 I always find that time seems to pass very quickly
7 At the start of the lesson she gave me books to pass
8 You don't have to be religious to tell the difference
9 My mother has been made vice-president
10 The building is now offices, but it was a bank

a between right and wrong.
b really embarrassing.
c to pass the ball.
d with a shaved head.
e to lock the door.
f around the class.
g of the company.
h in former times.
i from the Bible.
j in the holidays.

5 Words and phrases → (p. 59)

1 I took off my clothes, ________ them, and put them on the bed. ________

2 Mum always wears clothes that ________. They look great on her! ________

3 The spider caught ________ in its ________. ________

4 The thieves told him to ________ ________ his money. ________

5 The ________ was terrible in the tropics, over 40°. ________

6 A cold ________ is often the sign that you are afraid. ________

7 I like ________ maths ________ French. I think they're both boring. ________

8 Nobody likes people who ________. It's not fair to the other players. ________

9 S________ it was such a nice day, we went for a walk. ________

10 The singer wore a skirt that was hardly ________. It was very short! ________

11 Is money the only thing that ________? Or is happiness more important? ________

12 The ________ ________ in the building are very old. ________

13 – Yes, they might ________ at any moment, and then we would all be wet. ________

anständig • aushändigen • da • falten • Fliege • Hitze • platzen • schummeln • Schweiß • Spinnennetz • Wasserrohr • weder … noch • wichtig sein • zusammenpassen

6 Q & A

Match the two parts of these dialogues.

1 What matters most to you?
2 What's the easiest way of getting good results?
3 You look all wet. Have you been swimming?
4 I know this skirt is short, but do you like it?
5 Do you sometimes think Jane is a spider?
6 What do you want me to do with these clothes?
7 What do you think of my new socks and shoes?
8 Can you lend me a little money?
9 All their songs sound identical to me – do you agree?
10 We're not used to heat like this at this time of year, are we?
11 What happened when they told you to give them your money?
12 What's that noise? Is it a ghost!?

a Fold them and put them away.
b Well, it's decent – just!
c Well, similar anyway.
d Since it's you, OK.
e Well, I didn't hand it over. I ran!
f Well, it's not by cheating.
g No, this is sweat!
h That's global warming for you.
i Don't be silly. It's the water pipes.
j Yes, and Ken is a fly in her web.
k Friends and family, I reckon.
l Nice. They match.

7 Words and phrases ➜ (pp. 60–61)

1 He's got a real ________ for languages and can speak ten. ________________

2 Does ________________ always lead to success? Do you have to be clever? ________________

3 This pen was a ______ from my aunt. She gave it to me in 2011. ________________

4 Billy still believes in ________ ________. That's why he gets so many presents. ________________

5 After looking around the shop for an hour, I p________ an interesting book. ________________

6 The car didn't stop at the s____________. You must always stop if it's red. ________________

7 How would you describe your own ____________? Do you know yourself? ________________

8 She was hurt, but she was ________ and didn't cry. ________________

9 Sportspeople are normally ________________. They want to do their best. ________________

10 My dad is ________ ________ old jazz music. He plays it all the time. ________________

11 Kim is a good friend. He's very ______. ________________

12 What were your ____________ before the test? Were you worried? ________________

13 Our teacher has a good ________ ____ __________. We laugh a lot. ________________

14 I think that being fair is an important __________. ________________

Ampel • auswählen • Charakter • Eigenschaft • Gefühl • Geschenk • Humor • Intelligenz • leistungsorientiert • loyal • Talent • tapfer • verrückt nach • Weihnachtsmann

8 That's wrong!

Circle the mistake(s) in each line and write the correct word(s) on the right. Two lines are correct – which?

1 He always makes me laugh. He's got a great sens of houmor. ________________

2 Good atheletes want to win. They're very competetive. ________________

3 My favourite charakter in the extract was the brav girl. ________________

4 In sport tallent is more important than inteligence. ________________

5 It's embarassing to make the identic mistake twice. ________________

6 He's a very dezent person, even with people he disagrees with. ________________

7 I don't think you can achieve anything by cheating. ________________

8 He liked niether the heat or the flies in Australia. ________________

9 One of the baskets on the cort needs to be repared. ________________

10 Your honest opinion really matters to us, said the vice-president. ________________

9 Words and phrases ➜ (pp. 61–62)

1 There's a ______________ shop I like very much. It's very special to me.	______________
2 He was very ______________ with his time. He took fours hours to help me.	______________
3 I'm __________________, but you are ______. I work a lot; you don't.	______________
4 It was very ________ of you to say that. It hurt me.	______________
5 You have to be ____________ ____ others. Accept them as they are.	______________
6 You can use ____________ like "-ness" to make nouns from adjectives.	______________
7 "Good" and "bad" are words of ____________ meaning.	______________
8 I don't ____________ this place. Where are we?	______________
9 I never make ______________ about exams. You never know what's coming.	______________
10 Roads are divided into different ______________ in my country.	______________
11 I enjoy ____________ and I love __________ when my friend reads to me.	______________

bestimmte(r, s) • entgegengesetzt • erkennen • faul • fleißig • gemein • großzügig • Kanufahren • Kategorien • Lyrik • Nachsilbe • tolerant gegenüber • Voraussage

10 Three into one

Join the three parts (one from each column) to make sentences.

1 There's no	a crazy	I salary, but we work hard for it.
2 Yesterday I had a	b brave	II supporter of the local team.
3 Not everyone is as	c scientific	III situation that I went bright red.
4 We get a very	d lazy	IV of you to go skydiving.
5 I come from a	e religious	V family where we all have two jobs.
6 My brother was very	f particular	VI evening watching TV at home.
7 Gabriella has always been a	g generous	VII methods to find criminals.
8 I think it was very	h hard-working	VIII to me when we were young.
9 Everyone in my family is	i tolerant	IX reason I don't like him. I just don't.
10 Different people have different	j loyal	X of people's differences as you, unfortunately.
11 The police use	k mean	XI about watersports, especially canoeing.
12 I found it such an	l embarrassing	XII beliefs. That's life.

11 Words and phrases ➜ (p. 64)

1 Do you like doing scientific ________________? ________________

2 I was ill with a ______ when I was on holiday. ________________

3 The doctors are trying to ___________ the illness. ________________

4 ____ ______ money I have, ____ ________ I am. ________________

5 Can you imagine life before ________________? How did things stay cold? ________________

6 Scientists spend lots of time in the ____. ________________

7 I want to work for an international ___________ or organization. ________________

8 He __________ to work on Sundays. He said he had to go to church. ________________

9 I need these __________ for my scientific experiment. ________________

10 We ran fast and arrived ___ ______ ____ the start of the match. ________________

Chemikalie • desto glücklicher • diagnostizieren • Experiment • Firma • je mehr • Kühlung • Labor • rechtzeitig • sich weigern • Virus

12 Almost the same

Match the sentences with similar meanings.

1 I asked him but he said no and that was that.
2 He said he needed it as quickly as possible.
3 He promised he wouldn't be late.
4 He's really hard-working.
5 He says everyone is different and you have to accept it.
6 He looks completely different these days.
7 His kitchen has flooded.
8 He always makes me laugh.
9 He's very generous. He gave it to me.
10 He was the one who chose the restaurant.
11 He runs his own company.
12 He spends all his money on travel.

a You certainly couldn't call him lazy.
b I nearly didn't recognise him.
c He's crazy about it.
d He picked where to eat.
e He said he'd be there in time.
f It was a gift.
g He simply refused.
h He's got a great sense of humour.
i He's very tolerant.
j He said the sooner, the better.
k His water pipes have burst.
l He has no boss.

13 Words and phrases ➜ (p. 64)

1 She likes sport but her real ____________ is music.	____________
2 The little idea slowly ______________ into a big project.	____________
3 Her ____________ boyfriend is called John. They've been together for three days.	____________
4 I have to ___________ my work to my teacher by next Monday.	____________
5 Book ________ take place in Frankfurt and Leipzig every year.	____________
6 The price ___________ travel and hotel costs, but not food.	____________
7 I want to study ____________ at university, then become a doctor.	____________
8 Modern cities _______ ____ Berlin and London are really cool.	____________
9 Without ______________ you achieve nothing.	____________

aktueller • beinhalten • einreichen • Leidenschaft • Medizin • Messe • Motivation • sich entwickeln • wie etwa

14 Quiz time!

1 What are "-ness", "-ity" and "-ence" at the end of words? ____________

2 What do you call someone who has no hair? ____________

3 Young children think this person brings them gifts in December. ____________

4 The hobby of jumping out of a plane. ____________

5 The opposite of accept. ____________

6 The second-most important person after the president of a company. ____________

7 If you get a bad result in a test. ____________

8 What's the fourth word? Swimming: pool, basketball: … ____________

9 What people who want to be doctors study. ____________

10 The liquid your body produces when it is very hot. ____________

11 Something you say about what you think will happen in the future. ____________

12 Ebola is an example. ____________

13 Love and hate are examples. ____________

14 Where can scientists work? ____________

15 Words and phrases ➜ (p. 65)

1 My sister used to have a ________ as a pet. She called him Jerry. ________

2 The appearance of animals changes over time. That's ________. ________

3 So, how are you going to ________ the problem? Will you be able to solve it? ________

4 We're learning all about hair in ________ this week. ________

5 There's an ________ number of boys and girls in our class: 14 and 14. ________

6 Bears don't feel the cold; their ________ is very warm and ________. ________

7 We will find the answer. This isn't a ________ ________. ________

8 The lab is closed. They're ________ it ________. It's going to be white. ________

9 This is no problem ____ ____ ____ ____. We'll solve it tomorrow. ________

10 Super! You show a good ________ of the topic. ________

Biologie • dick • Evolution • Fell • gleiche • in Angriff nehmen • langfristig • Maus • Sackgasse • streichen • Verständnis

16 One from two

Decide which word completes the sentence.

1 It's more than a hobby for me. It's an absolute
2 We will all see the advantages of this in the long
3 We learn about nature and how the body works in
4 Species have changed over time. That's
5 I don't like to eat foods that have been grown using
6 I went to talk to a lot of different companies at the job
7 The work we did wasn't useful. We went down a blind
8 I don't think people should wear clothes made from
9 For the scientific experiment they used a white
10 You won't get anywhere in life or sport without

a biology
b fair
c evolution
d fur
e term
f mouse
g passion
h motivation
i chemicals
j alley

17 Words and phrases ➜ *(pp. 65–68)*

1 I understand the __________ of evolution now.	__________
2 I ____ think exam results are important, really.	__________
3 Some people will do anything to __________ in life.	__________
4 The results of the test will be __________ tomorrow.	__________
5 I don't plan things. I like to be __________.	__________
6 When I was young, I loved ________ stories like *Peter Pan*.	__________
7 This chapter __________ on evolution and is very interesting.	__________
8 The police __________ the area for clues for three days.	__________
9 You should ______ your work every 10 minutes.	__________

bekanntgeben • durchsuchen • Erfolg haben • Piraten • Prinzip • sich konzentrieren • speichern • spontan • wirklich

18 Missing!

Add words to two of the three gaps in each line.

1 Having relevant ______ experience makes ______ huge difference when ______ comes to applying for jobs.

2 I need ______ money so I want to find a job, and ______ sooner ______ better.

3 ______ languages ______ as English and Spanish ______ spoken all over the world.

4 I don't know why my sister wants to be ______ doctor. ______ Mum nor Dad are in ______ medicine.

5 It's important to ______ spontaneous, but in the ______ term, success comes from ______ planning.

6 You might not think ______ , but I really ______ want your project to ______ succeed.

7 My hair is in ______ eyes. It's ______ too long now. I think I'll ______ it cut at the weekend.

8 Before I book a holiday, I want ______ know ______ exactly what's ______ in the price.

9 Dad is often away with his ______ business, but he always comes back ______ time ______ Christmas.

10 In addition to ______ good understanding of people, you need ______ a good sense ______ humour in this job.

19 Words and phrases ➔ (pp. 68–70)

1 I ________ myself ____ one hour of TV a day. ____________

2 Not so fast! Think ____________ before you give the answer. ____________

3 The Italians ____________ a lot of wine, and drink quite a lot too. ____________

4 What's the __________ of your information? Where did you get it? ____________

5 I won't go to the party _________ you go too. Please come. ____________

6 She __________ Shakespeare in her work. It was something from *Hamlet*. ____________

7 These are English ____________ __________ : "…" ____________

8 British people use more ____________ than Germans when they speak. ____________

9 Our football club has a __________ called "Ritter Keule". ____________

10 I'm planning to run a ____________ this year. It's my first time to do 42 km. ____________

Anführungszeichen • außer • Handbewegung • herstellen • Marathon • Maskottchen • Quelle • sich auf etwas begrenzen • sorgfältig • zitieren

20 Scrambled report

Put the parts in the correct order. The first one has been done for you.

a People say it's important to aim high in life and work hard to

b in a band. As for me, what I want more than anything else is to be

c the ball after school and when we are playing another team in a school

n to me. My friends tell me I have the right qualities: neither motivation

d favourite is basketball. I feel completely at home when I am on the

g as wanting to start their own business, or to be a film star and work

h dreams come true it's better to take small steps than to expect to

i nor hard work are a problem for me. Things are going well now. To

f in Hollywood. Another of my friends from school just wants to play

l succeed immediately. Some of my friends have ambitions such

m court, both when we are practising something like passing

j date we have won all our matches, and that has increased our confidence

o competition. I am quite competitive, and winning really matters

k a professional basketball player. All sports are great, but my particular

e achieve your goals, which makes sense. They also say to make big

Answer: a ☐ ☐ ☐ ☐ ☐ ☐ ☐ ☐ ☐ ☐ ☐ ☐ ☐ ☐

21 Words and phrases ➜ (p. 70)

1 Your button is coming off. It needs to be ______ back on. ____________

2 I don't want a boring job. I want one where I can be ______. ____________

3 I'll do it, I promise. You can ______ ______ me. ____________

4 If you want to know more, please ______ us for more details. ____________

5 Lots of houses were ______ in the storm. ____________

6 His money is in a ______ until he's 18. Then he will be rich! ____________

7 My uncle ______ old cars. It takes a lot of time, but they look great. ____________

annähen • beschädigen • kreativ • restaurieren • sich auf jn. verlassen • sich bei jm. melden • Stiftung

22 Fill the gaps

Use one word from each of two boxes (**A + B**, **A + C**, or **B + C**) to complete each of these sentences.

A
do • focus • gesture • rely • tell • unless

B
not • on • principles • refused • restored • science • too

C
again • carefully • lab • on • since • marathon • work

1 Young children ______ ______ their parents for everything. That's natural.

2 They're having the chairs and sofas ______ so they can use them ______.

3 I couldn't run a ______; it's just ______ far for me.

4 This year I need to ______ ______ getting the best possible exam results.

5 Our ______ lessons are normally in the ______.

6 You can ______ when someone is competitive from the way they ______.

7 I'm ______ going to tell you ______ you ask.

8 Let me know if you ______ decide to go ______ I've heard the film is worth seeing.

9 I'm going to explain the ______ of the trust, so listen ______.

10 The police officer made a ______ at the driver to stop but the driver ______.

23 Words and phrases ➜ (pp. 70–71)

1 Over a hundred ______ applied for the job. ______

2 A ______ tells the story of your life at work. ______

3 How much ______ information is necessary? My parents' jobs? ______

4 In a ______ ______ you talk about your strengths and interests. ______

5 The president made a ______ on the radio. ______

6 Which ______ will you vote for in the election? ______

7 Give the ______ of your work experience, with month and year. ______

8 Put them in ______ order, so end with the oldest. ______

9 The book uses ______ I don't understand. I need a dictionary! ______

10 This CV still has mistakes in it. Have you had it ______? ______

11 Which is your favourite ______ in your hometown? ______

12 It's expensive here! House prices have ______ a lot. ______

Begriff • Bewerber • Datum • Erklärung • Kandidat/in • Korrektur lesen • Lebenslauf • Motivationsschreiben • persönlich • steigen • umgekehrt • Viertel

24 A conversation about CVs

Put the replies in this dialogue in the correct order.

1 What are the most important things to include in a CV? I've never written one before.

2 So should I include all the exams I passed and failed from primary school?

3 Right. And do I put in details of the hobbies I enjoy?

4 What about things such as relaxing, watching TV and playing video games?

5 You mean, a sentence or two to show I'm someone with motivation and qualities like that?

6 Right, so I shouldn't make things up, you mean?

7 Finally, what sort of experience do you think is important to include?

a I'd leave them out, to be honest. And you need to write a personal statement.

b Yes, especially things like team sports because that could be releavant to the jobs you want.

c Absolutely. You wouldn't cheat in an exam, so you must also stick to the truth on your CV.

d Well, if you've been a volunteer, or looked after children – things that show you are a responsible person.

e No, I'd focus on secondary school. And just put the main ones, like the *Abitur*, of course.

f Exactly. But make sure they are true because if you have an interview they will ask you about that.

g Well, start with your education and the subjects you studied at school, and your qualifications.

25 Words and phrases ➜ (p. 71)

1 You need a ____________ of biology to be a doctor. ____________

2 We've sold over 2 million books ____ ______. That's in only two weeks! ____________

3 If he's 11, is he already at ____________ school? ____________

4 Or does he still go to __________ school? ____________

5 Did you get a ______________ from the course? It's useful for later. ____________

6 I like old-fashioned hobbies like sewing and ______ ______. ____________

7 The course was 1 year. After ____________ of the course I soon found a job. ____________

8 Lots of young people love computers and want to work in ___. ____________

9 I'm reading a book about ________ history. No, it's not in Latin! ____________

Abschluss • bis heute • Filzen • Grundschule • IT • Kenntnisse • Qualifikation • römisch • weiterführende Schule

26 The right word

Circle the correct word to complete the sentences.

1 We got a qualification on **complete** • **completed** • **completion** of the course.

2 The quality of the **applied** • **applicants** • **application** was really high.

3 I don't know very much about **Rome** • **Roman** • **Romanish** architecture.

4 Her **knowledge** • **knowing** • **know** of biology is very impressive.

5 I've never **sewn** • **sewing** • **sew** a button on a shirt before.

6 These are his words, so put them in **quotation** • **quote** • **quoted** marks.

7 I made a **spontan** • **spontaning** • **spontaneous** decision to walk into the cinema.

8 Because she reacted quickly, she managed to **safe** • **save** • **saved** his life.

9 My dream job would be one where I can be **create** • **creative** • **creating** .

10 I don't like having to rely **in** • **on** • **with** other people.

11 Be calm. Don't let your **quality** • **emotion** • **talent** control how you think.

12 I spent hours **proofreading** • **proofingread** • **proofingreading** my CV.

13 What's your **person** • **personal** • **personally** opinion about cheating?

14 Animals are protected from the cold by their **big** • **fat** • **thick** fur.

Lösungen

Volume 5: Unit 1

1 Words and phrases

1 region 2 bush 3 coral 4 kangaroo 5 outback 6 spiders 7 coastal 8 exotic 9 humid 10 remote 11 stunning 12 tropical 13 tropics 14 urban

2 The right words

1 tropical; stunning 2 humid; tropics 3 kangaroos; exotic 4 remote; outback 5 spiders; urban

3 Words and phrases

1 Aboriginal 2 camel 3 convicts 4 Koalas 5 poisonous 6 exchange 7 flight 8 lively 9 historical 10 quarter 11 settled 12 trendy 13 business district

4 Match the parts

1 c 2 a 3 e 4 j 5 g 6 d 7 i 8 b 9 f 10 h

5 Words and phrases

1 flying fox 2 foxes 3 opera 4 quay 5 half-hour 6 two-week 7 waterfront 8 guided 9 honest 10 take 11 Catch

6 Wrong!

1 ten-hour/remotest 2 trendy/quarter 3 convicts 4 coastal/coral 5 kangaroos/camels 6 exotic/poisonous 7 *correct* 8 Opera 9 business/attractions 10 *correct* 11 honest/urban 12 Aboriginal

7 Words and phrases

1 scenic 2 transformed 3 landmark 4 paradise 5 bay 6 Back then 7 Aussie 8 were 9 though 10 barbecue/barbie 11 board 12 swallow 13 tons 14 private

8 Fitting everything together

1 ~~stunning~~ private 2 ~~catch~~ transform 3 ~~paradise~~ landmark 4 ~~private~~ stunning 5 ~~surfer's board~~ paradise 6 ~~landmark~~ board 7 ~~tons~~ barbecues 8 ~~barbecues~~ tons 9 ~~swallow~~ catch 10 ~~transform~~ swallow

9 Words and phrases

1 accepted 2 talkative 3 photography 4 in the end 5 was; homesick 6 Christmas Eve 7 self-confident 8 easy-going 9 very first 10 sunscreen

10 Three into one

1 e+VI 2 g+IV 3 a+I 4 b+VII 5 f+II 6 h+III 7 c+VIII 8 d+V

11 Quick quiz

1 barbie 2 Aussie 3 Christmas Eve 4 sunscreen 5 photography

12 Words and phrases

1 No worries 2 mates 3 Argumentative; arguments 4 argumentative writing 5 argued 6 brainstorm 7 oppose 8 stating 9 abroad 10 In addition to 11 Personally 12 discuss

13 Almost the same

1 h 2 e 3 j 4 a 5 b 6 g 7 c 8 d 9 f 10 i

14 Words and phrases

1 Furthermore 2 in my view 3 On the one hand 4 On the other hand 5 take a different view 6 advantage 7 disadvantage 8 make comparisons 9 To start/begin with 10 Firstly 11 Secondly 12 Thirdly

15 Fill the gaps

1 addition to 2 in; view 3 other hand 4 take view 5 the tropics 6 settled in 7 Back then 8 To; with

16 Words and phrases

1 reef 2 flooded 3 determined to 4 insects 5 python 6 Luckily 7 prefer; to; humans 8 mainly 9 provoke 10 injured; moths 11 crocodiles 12 bump into 13 snorkelled

17 Talking about presentations

1 e 2 h 3 a 4 g 5 c 6 j 7 d 8 i 9 f 10 b

18 Words and phrases

1 greenhouse 2 coastline 3 dramatic 4 facilities are 5 overcrowded 6 Rural 7 Suburban 8 vast 9 inland 10 mild 11 mountainous 12 old-fashioned 13 flat 14 descriptive 15 Collocations

19 Keywords

Suggestions: 1 a 24-hour supermarket. 2 your take on the plan? 3 great idea in my view. 4 my very first time abroad. 5 determined to win. 6 take a different view.

20 Words and phrases

1 disagree 2 rude; hurtful 3 nonsense 4 share 5 totally 6 I'm afraid 7 have a point 8 gift token 9 So can 10 So does 12 So would

21 Scrambled report

1 a 2 e 3 g 4 c 5 j 6 f 7 i 8 d 9 l 10 k 11 b 12 h 13 m

22 Words and phrases

1 sort of 2 soccer 3 is digging 4 opportunity 5 possibility 6 work experience 7 clinic 8 patients 9 debated 10 racism 11 racist 12 professional

23 Missing!

1 –/–/of/to 2 the/of/–/– 3 –/who/that so/– 4 –/with/–/a 5 –/–/with/are 6 –/an/the/– 7 –/as/–/in 8 –/to/–/would

24 Words and phrases

1 swans 2 medal 3 award 4 stood up for 5 recognition 6 stand against 7 was named 8 criticized for 9 opposing 10 apes 11 row 12 upset

25 More about Sydney

1 Aboriginal 2 tools 3 human 4 capital 5 natural 6 waterfront 7 attraction 8 settled 9 transformed 10 convicts 11 population 12 abroad 13 business 14 foreign 15 events 16 addition 17 landmarks

26 Words and phrases

1 victory 2 comment 3 innocent 4 put blame on; for 5 Unfortunately 6 bullied 7 appearance 8 industry 9 society 10 incident 11 booed 12 achievement 13 series 14 setting

27 The right word

1 medal 2 opposing 3 row 4 Unfortunately 5 stand up for 6 stand against 7 lively 8 take 9 hurtful 10 overcrowded

28 Crossword

Across: 1 mate 3 quarter 8 camel 10 injured 12 remote 14 overcrowded 15 sunscreen 19 snorkel 21 appearance 22 collocation 23 oppose
Down: 2 transform 4 spider 5 greenhouse 6 trendy 7 private 8 criticize 9 python 11 barbie 12 rude 13 crocodile 16 soccer 17 kangaroo 18 coastline 19 swan 20 stunning 24 patient

Volume 5: Unit 2

1 Words and phrases

1 photographer 2 novel 3 reckon 4 promise 5 salty 6 treated 7 haircut 8 That's fine by me 9 vote; elections 10 subject; politics 11 sensitive 12 issue 13 Once 14 waste

2 The right words

1 promise; novel; once 2 politics; subject 3 haircut; reckon 4 vote; fine 5 elections; waste 6 sensitive; treat

3 Words and phrases

1 tree trunk 2 chin; tore 3 keys 4 shook 5 first aid 6 breathe 7 skin 8 cheeks 9 pulse 10 brain; oxygen 11 distant 12 sink 13 intelligent 14 occasionally

4 Logic!

1 h 2 f 3 i 4 a 5 b 6 j 7 g 8 d 9 e 10 c

5 Words and phrases

1 dreamy 2 immigrants 3 university 4 soap; deodorant 5 toothbrush 6 toothpaste 7 fridge; can(s) 8 pretty; anyway 9 familiar 10 awkward 11 next door

6 Missing!

1 deodorant 2 university 3 awkward 4 sensitive 5 toothpaste 6 occasionally 7 immigrants 8 breathe 9 familiar 10 oxygen

7 Words and phrases

1 muscles 2 hands 3 meant 4 because of 5 serious 6 first-person narratives 7 request 8 informal 9 attracted to 10 fell in love; dated 11 is seeing 12 broken up 13 got to know 14 annoyed with

8 That's wrong!

1 promise; sensitive 2 arguing; waste 3 toothpaste 4 meant; forgot 5 narratives; university 6 Occasionally; intelligent 7 muscles; oxygen 8 *correct* 9 staring; dreamy 10 shaking; haircut

9 Words and phrases

1 confused 2 cross with 3 frightened 4 hopeful 5 Hopefully 6 pessimistic 7 pleased 8 furious with 9 heartbroken 10 is terrified of

10 Three into one

1 j+V 2 g+IX 3 a+VII 4 f+XI 5 c+VIII 6 h+VI 7 i+II 8 k+I 9 l+XII 10 d+X 11 b+III 12 e+IV

11 Words and phrases

1 thrilled 2 absolutely 3 ex- 4 male; female 5 acquaintance 6 enter 7 password 8 updated; status 9 account

12 Almost the same

1 j 2 i 3 b 4 d 5 h 6 a 7 k 8 e 9 f 10 c 11 l 12 g

13 Words and phrases

1 murder **2** declared **3** husband; wife **4** ought to **5** diet **6** diet **7** protein **8** healthy **9** supposed to **10** pasta **11** cultural **12** communication

14 Quiz time!

1 fridge **2** husband **3** soap **4** account **5** female **6** pasta **7** informal **8** novel **9** tree trunk **10** murder **11** chin **12** password

15 Words and phrases

1 statistics **2** Bar charts **3** Pie charts **4** chart **5** average **6** length **7** useful **8** percentage **9** chores **10** realized **11** insists on

16 One from two

1 f **2** i **3** g **4** a **5** k **6** h **7** b **8** e **9** l **10** d **11** c **12** j

17 Words and phrases

1 amount **2** values **3** tidy **4** cash **5** simply **6** running out of **7** encourage; perhaps **8** Certain habits **9** agreement **10** express **11** stress **12** hens **13** agreed **14** remind

18 Missing!

1 an/–/–/to **2** –/on/the, their/– **3** –/a/–/by **4** a, the/–/was, is/– **5** at/for/–/– **6** –/with/the/– **7** –/–/of/at **8** to/–/a/–

19 Words and phrases

1 refugee **2** youth **3** organization **4** run **5** published **6** friendship **7** fill in; form **8** distance

20 Scrambled report

1 a **2** h **3** f **4** k **5** d **6** i **7** e **8** n **9** g **10** l **11** c **12** b **13** m **14** j **15** o

21 Words and phrases

1 transport **2** he faced **3** fit in **4** Act **5** adapt **6** got used to **7** ended up

22 Keywords

Mögliche Lösungen: **1** We've run out of eggs. **2** He reminded me it was her birthday. **3** I'm on a diet. **4** The distance between the Moon and the Earth is about 400,000 km. **5** It was cold, but we went for a swim in the sea anyway. **6** My parents didn't like the length of my hair. **7** At first I didn't like the hotel, but now I've got used to it. **8** We ended up having an argument. **9** We are facing a big problem. **10** I only have a small amount of money.

23 Words and phrases

1 responsibility **2** within **3** advisor **4** carer **5** dependent on **6** got to see **7** didn't; anywhere

24 A conversation

1 e **2** a **3** f **4** c **5** d **6** b

25 Words and phrases

1 shop window **2** apron **3** are; in; a hurry **4** normally **5** stiff **6** including **7** tandem **8** hub **9** handmade

26 The right word

1 cross **2** normally **3** salty **4** know **5** haircuts **6** update **7** including **8** next **9** is; it **10** fill **11** a **12** protein

27 Dialogues

1 f **2** j **3** g **4** l **5** b **6** k **7** d **8** a **9** e **10** h **11** c **12** i

28 Missing!

1 first **2** dependent **3** heartbroken **4** windows **5** Hopefully **6** transport **7** advisor/adviser; encourage **8** agreement **9** remind; organization **10** normally; friendships

Volume 5: Unit 3

1 Words and phrases

1 army **2** athlete **3** global warming **4** make a difference **5** repaired **6** scientific **7** skydiving **8** achieved **9** goals **10** deadline **11** failed **12** application **13** applied for

2 The right words

1 scientific; global warming **2** applying; army **3** goal; skydiving **4** difference; athletes **5** achieved; application **6** fail; repaired **7** deadline; applications

3 Words and phrases

1 excerpt **2** vice **3** former **4** about to **5** court **6** identical **7** shaved **8** pass **9** Bible; religious **10** bald **11** tell **12** embarrassing

4 Match the parts

1 e **2** d **3** i **4** b **5** c **6** j **7** f **8** a **9** g **10** h

5 Words and phrases

1 folded **2** match **3** flies; web **4** hand over **5** heat **6** sweat **7** neither; nor **8** cheat **9** Since **10** decent **11** matters **12** water pipes **13** burst

6 Q&A

1 k **2** f **3** g **4** b **5** j **6** a **7** l **8** d **9** c **10** h **11** e **12** i

7 Words and phrases

1 talent **2** intelligence **3** gift **4** Santa Claus **5** picked **6** stoplight **7** character **8** brave **9** competitive **10** crazy about **11** loyal **12** emotions **13** sense of humour **14** quality

8 That's wrong!

1 sense/humour 2 athletes/competitive 3 character/brave 4 talent/intelligence 5 embarrassing/ identical 6 decent 7 *correct* 8 neither/nor 9 court/repaired 10 *correct*

9 Words and phrases

1 particular 2 generous 3 hard-working; lazy 4 mean 5 tolerant of 6 suffixes 7 opposite 8 recognize 9 predictions 10 categories 11 canoeing; poetry

10 Three into one

1 f+IX 2 d+VI 3 t+X 4 g+I 5 h+V 6 k+VIII 7 j+II 8 b+IV 9 a+XI 10 e+XII 11 c+VII 12 l+III

11 Words and phrases

1 experiments 2 virus 3 diagnose 4 The more; the happier 5 refrigeration 6 lab 7 company 8 refused 9 chemicals 10 in time for

12 Almost the same

1 g 2 j 3 e 4 a 5 i 6 b 7 k 8 h 9 f 10 d 11 l 12 c

13 Words and phrases

1 passion 2 developed 3 current 4 submit 5 fair 6 includes 7 medicine 8 such as 9 motivation

14 Quiz time!

1 suffixes 2 bald 3 Santa Claus 4 skydiving 5 refuse 6 vice-president 7 fail 8 court 9 medicine 10 sweat 11 prediction 12 virus 13 emotion 14 lab/laboratory

15 Words and phrases

1 mouse 2 evolution 3 tackle 4 biology 5 equal 6 fur; thick 7 blind alley 8 having; painted 9 in the long term 10 understanding

16 One from two

1 g 2 e 3 a 4 c 5 i 6 b 7 j 8 d 9 f 10 h

17 Words and phrases

1 principle 2 do 3 succeed 4 announced 5 spontaneous 6 pirate 7 focuses 8 searched 9 save

18 Missing!

1 –/a/it 2 –/the/the 3 –/such/are 4 a/Neither/– 5 be/long/– 6 so/do/ – 7 my/–/have 8 to/–/included 9 –/in/for 10 a/–/of

19 Words and phrases

1 limit; to 2 carefully 3 produce 4 source 5 unless 6 quoted 7 quotation marks 8 gestures 9 mascot 10 marathon

20 Scrambled report

1 a 2 e 3 h 4 l 5 g 6 f 7 b 8 k 9 d 10 m 11 c 12 o 13 n 14 i 15 j

21 Words and phrases

1 sewn 2 creative 3 rely on 4 contact 5 damaged 6 trust 7 restores

22 Fill the gaps

1 rely; on 2 restored; again 3 marathon; too 4 focus; on 5 science; lab 6 tell; work 7 not; unless 8 do; since 9 principles; carefully 10 gesture; refused

23 Words and phrases

1 applicants 2 CV 3 personal 4 personal statement 5 statement 6 candidate 7 dates 8 reverse 9 terms 10 proofread 11 neighbourhood 12 increased

24 A conversation about CVs

1 g 2 e 3 b 4 a 5 f 6 c 7 d

25 Words and phrases

1 knowledge 2 to date 3 secondary 4 primary 5 qualification 6 felt craft 7 completion 8 IT 9 Roman

26 The right word

1 completion 2 applicants 3 Roman 4 knowledge 5 sewn 6 quotation 7 spontaneous 8 save 9 creative 10 on 11 emotion 12 proofreading 13 personal 14 thick

27 Keywords

Mögliche Lösungen: 1 Many people applied for the job. 2 At weekends, I limit the children to an hour a day on the computer. 3 He refuses to eat meat unless he knows where it's from. 4 The only way you can succeed in life is to work hard. 5 I like neither canoeing nor poetry. 6 There's an equal number of boys and girls in our class. 7 When my computer stopped working I had it repaired. 8 Illnesses such as the Ebola virus have killed many people. 9 Friday is the deadline for the project.

28 Missing!

1 knowledge; principles; refrigeration 2 personal; marathon 3 primary; secondary 4 neighbourhood; increased 5 statement; contribution; mascot 6 restoring; deadline

Volume 5: Unit 4

1 Words and phrases

1 issue 2 gap 3 gap year 4 scholarship 5 common 6 native languages 7 ranked 8 based on 9 in total 10 original 11 dubbed

2 Logic!

1 j 2 l 3 c 4 a 5 e 6 f 7 h 8 k 9 d
10 g 11 j 12 b

3 Words and phrases

1 stored **2** technical **3** dominant **4** aviation
5 navigation **6** diplomacy **7** interpret **8** contain
9 portraits **10** panorama **11** out of focus **12** Analyse

4 That's wrong!

1 scholarship **2** originally **3** aviation **4** portraits
5 technical **6** correct **7** panorama **8** focus
9 analyse **10** correct

5 Words and phrases

1 creates **2** comment on **3** come across **4** understood
5 paraphrase **6** slow down **7** difficulty **8** internship
9 spring break **10** accommodation

6 Three into one

1 d+n 2 b+l 3 c+t 4 e+f 5 j+m 6 a+s
7 h+o 8 g+p 9 f+r 10 i+q

7 Words and phrases

1 cycled **2** hiked **3** itinerary **4** luggage
5 baggage **6** suitcase **7** Flight attendants
8 customs **9** travel agent's **10** I'm leaving for

8 Logic!

1 e 2 j 3 h 4 a 5 l 6 d 7 k 8 c 9 f 10 i
11 b 12 g

9 Words and phrases

1 space **2** out of the blue **3** foreigners **4** via
5 backpackers **6** non- **7** sort of **8** organic farm
9 exam **10** by the time

10 The right words

1 backpacker; space **2** foreign **3** gap; farm **4** agent
5 sort; made/makes **6** exam; paraphrase **7** difficulty; internship **8** dominant; ranked **9** technical; store
10 comment; create

11 Words and phrases

1 overhead locker **2** beer **3** book **4** metro
5 Come by **6** shrugged **7** burst out laughing
8 plenty of **9** downside

12 Almost the same

1 e 2 i 3 k 4 b 5 j 6 d 7 a 8 g 9 l
10 c 11 f 12 h

3 The right little word

1 of **2** by **3** out **4** of **5** for **6** themselves
7 across **8** by **9** out **10** down

14 Scrambled story

1 a 2 f 3 k 4 e 5 j 6 l 7 b 8 g 9 i 10 c
11 m 12 d 13 h

15 Missing!

1 suitcases **2** downside **3** organic **4** paraphrase
5 originally **6** dominant **7** accommodation
8 contains **9** difficulty **10** overhead locker
11 backpacker **12** scholarship

16 The right word

1 technical **2** laughing **3** locker **4** customs
5 non- **6** issue **7** attendants **8** ranked **9** time
10 break **11** diplomacy

17 Crossword

Across: 2 itinerary **4** panorama **6** foreigners **8** exam
10 portrait **11** downside **12** shrug **17** scholarship
19 cycle **20** gap **21** navigation **22** metro
Down: 1 backpacker **3** paraphrase **5** dubbed
7 internship **9** accommodation **13** diplomacy
14 hike **15** dominant **16** baggage **18** suitcase
19 customs **23** rank

Volume 6: Unit 1

1 Words and phrases

1 teens **2** dreadlocks; curly **3** kinky; is; dressed
4 casually; blazer **5** denim **6** paint; headscarf **7** tie
8 unlike **9** mysterious **10** patriotic **11** hairstyle; suggest **12** thoughtful **13** conservative **14** original
15 prefer; to

2 Scrambled sentences

1 a 2 f 3 g 4 c 5 d 6 e 7 b

3 Words and phrases

1 poet **2** picture; routine **3** desires **4** painfully
5 cope; alarm **6** winked at; headphones **7** ignored; hood **8** instructor; simple **9** branch **10** records
11 makes **12** yet **13** Nor do **14** somewhat

4 Just the opposite

1 routine **2** ignore **3** simple **4** cope **5** original
6 desires **7** nor **8** instructor

5 Words and phrases

1 identity **2** perspective **3** circa; obvious
4 appeal to **5** reflects **6** imagery; types **7** Similes; metaphors **8** devices **9** gentle **10** dove
11 considered **12** consider **13** Hawks; owls

6 Three into one

1 j+n 2 g+s 3 a+p 4 c+k 5 h+o 6 i+t
7 b+q 8 e+l 9 d+m 10 f+r

7 Words and phrases

1 space 2 influenced 3 value 4 athletic 5 gay; straight 6 aggressive; ambitious 7 reliable 8 musical; passionate 9 conventional; liberal 10 African-American 11 upbringing 12 dialect; particularly 13 modify 14 weak 15 search engine

8 Wrong!

1 instructor 2 passionate 3 dialects 4 metaphor 5 athletic 6 correct 7 obvious 8 reliable 9 straight 10 correct

9 Words and phrases

1 basic 2 format; visual 3 proper 4 margin; indent 5 in relation to 6 font; italics 7 bold type; clarity 8 untidy; legible 9 point/pt.; function 10 type 11 opinion piece; gender 12 recognize 13 make up 14 nonexistent 15 differ; biological 16 when it comes to

10 The right word

1 Americans; up 2 gentle; when; aggressive 3 opinion; typed; search 4 font; indent; visual 5 gender; influence; upbringing 6 basic; differ; biologically

11 Words and phrases

1 representation 2 had 3 recently 4 show up 5 counsellor; ridiculous 6 contribution 7 entire 8 After all 9 constantly 10 eliminate 11 In the meantime 12 importance

12 Almost the same

1 f 2 c 3 e 4 a 5 i 6 g 7 j 8 d 9 h 10 b

13 Words and phrases

1 focus 2 examine 3 receive 4 options 5 headline; caught; attention 6 drew; attention to 7 provocative 8 solution to 9 back up 10 restate 11 calls for 12 sexes 13 marriage 14 paragraph break

14 Missing words

1 it/-/-/for 2 -/was/-/was 3 not/-/all/- 4 -/pay/-/type 5 -/in/to/- 6 the/-/have/- 7 -/up/-/is 8 -/in/-/to

15 Words and phrases

1 general 2 pay; workplace 3 discriminate against 4 sadly; take; time off 5 raise; voice 6 fine 7 take; unequal; seriously 8 persuasion 9 persuaded 10 anecdote; factual 11 expressive 12 Rhetorical 13 deny 14 emphatic

16 Missing parts

1 rhetorical 2 expressive 3 emphatic 4 persuasion 5 discriminate 6 seriously 7 provocative 8 attention 9 factual 10 options

17 Words and phrases

1 beyond 2 cell 3 genes; individual 4 human race 5 technology 6 ancient 7 rusted 8 erode 9 reduce; to 10 earthquake 11 species 12 records 13 were around 14 skeletons

18 The right word

1 fine 2 race 3 beyond 4 raise 5 around 6 quake 7 off 8 deny 9 pay 10 sadly

19 Words and phrases

1 astonishment 2 excitement 3 ups and downs 4 comprehension 5 power line 6 repairs 7 high winds 8 complete 9 yard 10 applause 11 climax 12 single; advertisement

20 More about writing

1 a 2 d 3 i 4 g 5 e 6 m 7 f 8 p 9 b 10 l 11 o 12 j 13 k 14 h 15 c 16 n 17 q

Volume 6: Unit 2

1 Words and phrases

1 pay rise 2 rise 3 define; meeting 4 jungle 5 locals 6 villagers; observed 7 affects; behaviour 8 drunk; relatives 9 Therefore 10 infected; cream 11 liquid 12 strolled 13 manners; no matter

2 Scrambled sentences

1 d 2 i 3 g 4 a 5 b 6 h 7 e 8 c 9 f

3 Words and phrases

1 happened to 2 on purpose 3 teach; lesson 4 trade(d); bullets 5 appropriate; greeting 6 respond 7 posts; turtles 8 the other day 9 sense 10 pole 11 came to an understanding 12 stingy 13 sandals; high heels 14 belly

4 Just the opposite

1 stingy 2 on purpose 3 the other day 4 responded 5 strolled 6 risen 7 sandals 8 belly 9 came to an understanding 10 relatives

5 Words and phrases

1 care for 2 beliefs 3 candy; mattress 4 reached for; unwrap 5 indicated 6 insulted 7 growth 8 giggle 9 shovel 10 with a straight face 11 analysis 12 bread rolls; and so on 13 Baltic Sea 14 lifted; catch; eye 15 staff; enthusiastic

6 Three into one

1 g+l 2 f+k 3 i+r 4 e+m 5 b+q 6 d+p 7 a+o 8 j+n 9 vc+s 10 h+t

7 Words and phrases

1 incredible 2 bank assistant; cyclist 3 tap water 4 embarrassed 5 violin 6 narration; footage 7 reflection 8 reviews 9 review; fictional 10 fiction; just as 11 misunderstanding 12 narrate; bathing 13 ignorant 14 put; off; for now 15 abandoned

8 Almost the same

1 e 2 i 3 b 4 j 5 a 6 h 7 c 8 f 9 d 10 g

9 Words and phrases

1 breastfeeding 2 eventually 3 literally 4 grew 5 enormous 6 informative 7 strongly 8 engaging 9 inform 10 plot 11 hint 12 summarize 13 summary 14 advanced 15 suitable

10 The right word

1 literally; insulted 2 summary; informative 3 suitable; plot 4 listening; advanced 5 strongly; breastfeeding 6 enormous; engaging 7 grow; eventually 8 incredible; violin

11 Words and phrases

1 ladder 2 genres 3 semi-autobiographical 4 crime; is set 5 effective; hilarious 6 moving; account 7 emphasis 8 emphasizes 9 highly; readable 10 entertaining 11 enjoyable 12 lifelike 13 gripping 14 meaningful 15 avoid

12 That's wrong

1 autobiographical; hilarious 2 emphasizes; read 3 set; gripping 4 correct 5 believe; lifelike 6 entertaining; genres 7 informative; breastfeeding 8 avoid; ladders 9 enormous; literally

13 Words and phrases

1 diversity 2 display 3 exhibition 4 harmony 5 embrace 6 derogatory 7 stereotype 8 present 9 captures 10 pasted 11 installed 12 participate in

14 Keywords

1 Over a million people signed the petition. 2 I haven't had a pay rise since at least three years ago. 3 I've decided to buy it, no matter how expensive it is. 4 He does things like that on purpose because he knows it annoys me. 5 Tomorrow's meeting has been put off until next Tuesday. 6 The reason he left early was in order to avoid the worst of the traffic.

15 Words and phrases

1 take a stand against/on 2 capital 3 virtual 4 march; projected 5 conference 6 dynamic 7 eerie 8 sight; haunting 9 soundtrack; surreal 10 politician 11 definitely; by 12 exercise 13 petrol/gas 14 gas station 15 attractive

16 Missing!

1 exercise 2 politicians 3 soundtrack 4 attractive 5 conference 6 capital 7 definitely 8 derogatory 9 participating

17 Words and phrases

1 political 2 involvement 3 got involved 4 activist; campaign 5 campaigned 6 citizens 7 democracy 8 initiative 9 MP 10 opinion poll 11 party 12 petition 13 policy

18 Scrambled sentences

1 a 2 e 3 g 4 j 5 h 6 f 7 c 8 l 9 i 10 k 11 b 12 d

19 Words and phrases

1 pressure group 2 referendum 3 safety 4 signature 5 signed 6 demand(ed) 7 elect 8 demonstrated 9 slide 10 aspects 11 forward(s) 12 infrastructure 13 fewer 14 low 15 synchronized

20 Quiz time!

1 gas 2 democracy 3 citizen 4 stereotypes 5 soundtrack 6 stroll 7 liquid 8 belly 9 therefore 10 fiction or fictional

21 Which verb?

1 kept 2 went 3 keep 4 took 5 made 6 came 7 took 8 went 9 make 10 came

22 Correcting compound nouns

1 high tap 2 race band 3 dairy power 4 tap search 5 opinion dairy 6 rubbish opinion 7 break race 8 search rubbish 9 power high 10 band break

Volume 6: Unit 3

1 Words and phrases

1 globe 2 technological progress 3 delivery 4 deliver; package 5 automation 6 Digital 7 drones; robots 8 artificial 9 bees; pollinate 10 pollen; agriculture 11 production 12 machine 13 replace 14 panel discussion

2 The right words

1 e 2 g 3 d 4 a 5 h 6 b 7 i 8 c 9 f

3 Words and phrases

1 benefits 2 benefit 3 risk 4 steam 5 cloth 6 innovation 7 nuclear; electricity 8 electric 9 vision 10 radioactive; waste 11 depend on 12 control 13 deals with 14 tone; concerned about

4 Scrambled sentences

1 i 2 f 3 h 4 a 5 e 6 c 7 j 8 d 9 b 10 g

5 Words and phrases

1 for instance 2 depicted 3 desperate 4 survival 5 poses a threat to 6 threatened 7 outweigh 8 vague 9 conscious 10 applications 11 nature; last 12 went on strike; cases 13 sequence 14 frequency 15 manner

6 Three into one

1 i/n 2 d/r 3 j/m 4 h/t 5 e/l 6 c/k 7 a/p 8 b/s 9 f/q 10 g/o

7 Words and phrases

1 manage 2 charge 3 swipe 4 battery 5 buttons; icons 6 menu; search bar 7 tabs 8 navigate 9 data; memory 10 run; delete 11 import; export 12 browsing 13 customize; settings 14 Attachments; blocks 15 friend request

8 Computer issues

1 browsing 2 friend request 3 delete 4 attachments 5 tabs 6 running 7 managed 8 import 9 battery 10 menu 11 customize 12 settings

9 Words and phrases

1 buzz off 2 feature article 3 trap 4 sting 5 harvest; crops 6 factors 7 use; pesticide(s) 8 varied; variety 9 Parasites; weaken 10 immune system; prone to 11 Hibernation 12 In addition

10 Almost the same

1 h 2 e 3 j 4 l 5 i 6 d 7 k 8 a 9 f 10 c 11 g 12 b

11 Words and phrases

1 shrunk 2 compensate 3 worrying; contribute 4 lay 5 recover 6 ensure; supplies 7 muesli 8 logical 9 generation 10 pilot; overall 11 effectiveness 12 disappearance 13 level 14 polar bear; organic

12 That's wrong!

1 organic 2 disappearance/worrying 3 ensure/laid 4 overall/effectiveness 5 correct 6 shrank 7 polar bear/recovering 8 logical/levels 9 correct 10 contributes

13 Words and phrases

1 economically; wordy 2 concise; impact 3 public; viewers 4 imagination 5 bankrupt; clerk 6 Customers; alternatives 7 hypothetical 8 curve 9 vertical 10 Civilization; smart 11 ratio 12 band 13 ruling

14 Missing!

1 bankrupt 2 alternatives 3 hypothetical 4 imagination 5 civilization 6 impact 7 spectator 8 customer 9 supplies 10 economically

15 Words and phrases

1 immortality 2 chews; put 3 accomplished 4 charming; glanced at 5 straightened 6 bomb 7 Cancer 8 possibly; analogy 9 physically 10 cushions 11 loose 12 privacy; romance 13 occur to 14 interior monologue 15 dozen

16 The right word

1 possibly 2 straightened 3 lose 4 privacy 5 feelings 6 romance 7 romance 8 interior 9 wordy 10 rules

17 Words and phrases

1 reasonable; sincerity 2 sincere; bright 3 beneath; hung up 4 springs 5 dialed; excuse 6 hesitate; exclusive 7 Netiquette; predict 8 similarly 9 direction; complain 10 gist; inferences

18 Scrambled sentences

1 a 2 k 3 i 4 b 5 g 6 e 7 h 8 j 9 c 10 l 11 f 12 d

19 Words and phrases

1 inferred 2 are likely to 3 explicitly 4 trust; admiration 5 admire; disrespect 6 affection 7 chairs; moderator 8 controversial 9 researching 10 ban 11 concerns 12 take sides 13 firmly 14 thorough 15 counter-arguments

21 Quiz time!

1 sting 2 pollen 3 steam 4 chew 5 cushion 6 vertical 7 curve

22 This person …

1 comedian 2 applicant 3 astronaut 4 campaigner 5 refugee 6 ancestor 7 cyclist 8 burglar

23 MENTal training

1 pavement 2 involvement 3 excitement 4 equipment 5 appointment 6 environment 7 astonishment 8 punishment

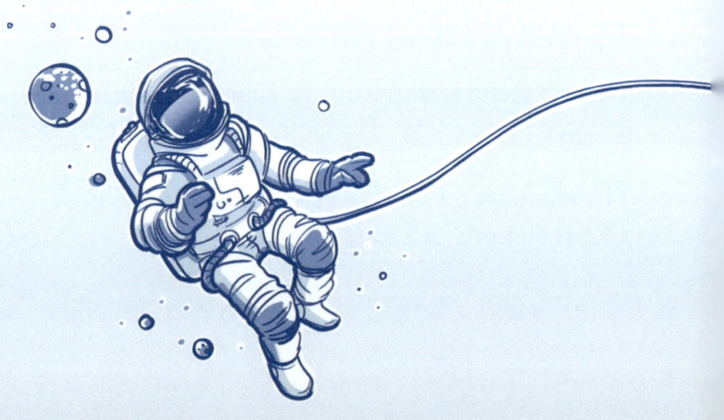

27 Keywords

Rewrite the sentences using the keywords so they mean the same as the original. Don't change the keyword in any way.

1 There were hundreds of applicants for the job. applied

Many people ______________________________.

2 I only allow the children to use the computer for an hour a day at the weekend. limit

At weekends, I ______________________________ on the computer.

3 He'll only eat meat if he knows where it comes from. unless

He refuses ______________________________ where it's from.

4 If you don't want to fail in life, you have to work hard. succeed

The only way ______________________________ work hard.

5 I don't like canoeing and I don't like poetry. nor

I like ______________________________.

6 We have ten girls and ten boys in our class. equal

There's ______________________________ boys and girls in our class.

7 I got someone to repair my computer for me. had

When my computer stopped working I ______________________________.

8 Many people have died because of things like the Ebola virus. as

Illnesses ______________________________ have killed many people.

9 We have to submit our project on Friday or before. deadline

Friday ______________________________ the project.

28 Missing!

Complete these sentences by writing in the missing words or parts of words.

1 His **know**__________ of the basic **princ**__________ of **refrig**__________ is impressive. He's an expert.

2 My **pers**__________ ambition is to run a **mara**__________ this year.

3 I didn't really enjoy **prim**__________ school, but __________ school was great.

4 The number of young families moving into this **neigh**__________ has **in**__________ a lot.

5 He made a __________**ment** about the value and **contri**__________ of the team **mas**__________.

6 He loves **re**__________ that old car so much that he won't set a **dead**__________ for finishing.

Connect through English

1 Words and phrases ➜ *(pp. 76–78)*

1 Where is this week's ________ of my football magazine? ____________________

2 There is the ______ in the fence. That's where the convict escaped. ____________________

3 Lots of people have a ______ ______ between school and university. ____________________

4 I got a ______________ to study here. It means I don't pay anything. ____________________

5 Malta, South Africa and Ireland have a ___________ language: English. ____________________

6 Mum is British and Dad is French, so I have two ________ __________. ____________________

7 We _________ the countries according to size, starting with the biggest. ____________________

8 My decision isn't spontaneous but is ________ ____ experience. ____________________

9 We lived there in 2011 and 2014, 13 months ___ ______. ____________________

10 I like watching films in the _________ language, not German. ____________________

11 But I need subtitles when the film isn't _________. ____________________

auf der Grundlage von • Ausgabe • gemeinsam • insgesamt • Jahr • Auszeit • Lücke • Muttersprache • ordnen • Original- • Stipendium • synchronisiert

2 Logic!

Match the two parts of these dialogues logically.

1 Carla's abroad now, isn't she?
2 Di Pietro. Are you from Italy?
3 Did you see the film in English?
4 Do you want me to make a list of restaurants?
5 Have you read the latest issue?
6 How are the hotels ranked on this list? Price?
7 I don't know the answer. Shall I leave a gap?
8 I've never heard that name before. Is it common?
9 Is the story an original one?
10 Isn't it expensive to study abroad?
11 So, you spent two years in New Zealand?
12 Your English is impressive!

a And rank them.
b Hope so. It's my native language.
c No, it was dubbed.
d No, it's based on Shakespeare.
e No, not yet.
f No. By size, I think.
g Not on a scholarship.
h Yes, do that.
i Yes, in total.
j Yes, on a gap year.
l Yes, originally.
k Yes, very.

3 Words and phrases ➜ (pp. 78–79)

1 The photos from our holiday are all __________ on this SD card. ____________________

2 As an engineer, Dad reads a lot of ____________ magazines. ____________________

3 Is China a ____________ world power? ____________________

4 I've got a book on the history of ____________. It starts with the Montgolfiers. ____________________

5 Ships rely on computers for ______________ on sea. ____________________

6 If you like languages and travel, work in ______________. ____________________

7 How would you ____________ this poem? What does it mean? ____________________

8 How much does this bottle __________? A litre, maybe? ____________________

9 Most of my photos are ____________ of my friends. ____________________

10 I went to the roof to see the _____________ of the city. ____________________

11 What's in this photo? It's _____ ____ ________. I can't see anything. ____________________

12 __________ what the picture below means to you. ____________________

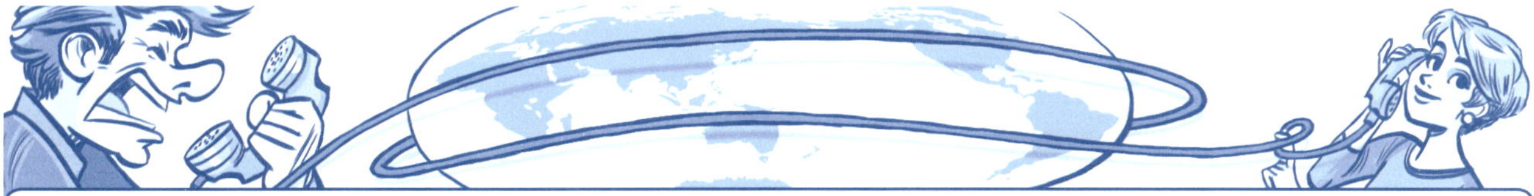

analysieren • Diplomatie • enthalten • interpretieren • Luftfahrt • Navigation • Panorama • Porträt • speichern • technisch • unscharf • vorherrschend

4 That's wrong!

Correct the mistakes in these sentences. Two lines are correct.

1 I was very lucky. I didn't have to pay because I won a sholarship. ____________________

2 We live in the capital now, but we are original from the country. ____________________

3 My brother's mad about flying. He wants to study avaition at university. ____________________

4 I have lots of portrats of people who work in diplomacy. ____________________

5 The technic information about navigation is difficult to understand. ____________________

6 What do you think is the dominant message of this photo? ____________________

7 My favourite photo was the panaroma of the city. It was beautiful. ____________________

8 The background of the photo was just a little out of focuss. ____________________

9 The teacher gave us a few pictures to analyze in detail. ____________________

10 I store all my documents on this disk. It contains everything. ____________________

5 Words and phrases ➜ *(pp. 79–81)*

1 The film's music is slow and dark. It ________ a scary atmosphere. ____________

2 May I ________ ____ your report? I need to talk about a few ideas. ____________

3 If you smile, you ______ ________ as friendly. ____________

4 I'm not perfect in Spanish, but I can make myself ____________. ____________

5 This is only a ____________ of what he said. The words were different. ____________

6 Not so fast! Please ______ ______ so I can understand you. ____________

7 I had __________ understanding the man. I think it was his regional accent. ____________

8 An __________ gives you practical experience. ____________

9 We're going to Florida in March for the ________ ______. ____________

10 Flats and other ______________ are quite expensive here. ____________

erschaffen • sich äußern • ankommen • verständlich • Umschreibung • langsamer werden • Schwierigkeiten • Praktikum • Frühjahrsferien • Unterkunft

6 Three into one

Match the three parts to make sentences.

1 These two suitcases here	a based	k a friendly atmosphere here.
2 Maybe it's not your plan, but you sometimes	b come	l across as rude.
3 The teacher asked us to	c comment	m down when speaking.
4 They use lights and colour to	d contain	n everything I own
5 If you want people to understand, you should	e create	o for cheap accommodation
6 We wrote a story that was	f dubbed	p for the spring break.
7 Around the train station is a good place to	g fly	q himself understood
8 New Zealand is great, but it's too far to	h look	r and not in the original language
9 Most foreign films are	i make	s on our time in Australia.
10 It was so loud the teacher had to shout to	j slow	t on the photo.

7 Words and phrases ➜ (p. 81)

1 The beach wasn't far and I had my bike, so I ________ there. ________________

2 They ________ in the mountains for a week and had very sore feet afterwards. ________________

3 What is the best ____________ for our holiday? Where shall we go first? ________________

4 What's the limit on ____________ with British Airways? ________________

5 I didn't take much ____________ out of the US. ________________

6 I just had one small ____________ with my clothes for the weekend. ________________

7 ________ ____________ always smile when you get on the plane. ________________

8 Are the ____________ in Wales different? Do the people do things differently? ________________

9 I bought my ticket at the ________ __________ in Church Road. ________________

10 I'___ __________ _____ Hollywood tomorrow in my private plane. ________________

abbrechen • Flugbegleiter/in • Gepäck (2 x) • Koffer • mit dem Rad fahren • Reisebüro • Reiseroute • Sitten • wandern

8 Logic!

Complete the sentences.

1 My sister works as a travel
2 If you need anything, our flight
3 In the US lots of students go away on spring
4 I can speak German, but it's not my native
5 The background is a little out of
6 I spent over €100 yesterday in
7 I prefer to see what happens, I never make a travel
8 It's our last day. Tomorrow we
9 In case you didn't understand, here's a
10 In Britain we say "luggage", but Americans say
11 I asked if he needed help because he was having
12 I know the company well because I did my

a language, so I make mistakes.
b difficulty reading the instructions.
c leave for home.
d total, which is a lot.
e agent in the city centre.
f paraphrase of what he said.
g internship there when I was a student.
h breaks to warm destinations.
i "baggage" instead.
j attendants are here to help.
k itinerary when I go abroad.
l focus so you can't see clearly.

9 Words and phrases ➜ (p. 82)

1 My suitcase is too small. I only have ________ for three pairs of shoes! ________

2 An old friend phoned Dad _____ _____ _____ _____ after 15 years. ________

3 A lot of ________ visit this area of the UK, but not many British people. ________

4 It was a strange itinerary: we went from Berlin to Hamburg _____ Munich. ________

5 We saw lots of ________ in India. They live and travel very simply. ________

6 Lots of ______ Italians live in this part of Italy, especially in the summer. ________

7 I ______ _____ see why Schalke are so popular, but I don't like them. ________

8 I buy my vegetables from an ________ ________. I don't like supermarkets. ________

9 I'm not coming tonight – I have an ________ tomorrow and need to revise. ________

10 Mum was asleep _____ _____ _____ I got home. ________

als • aus heiterem Himmel • Ausländer/in • Bio-Bauernhof • irgendwie • nicht- • Platz • Prüfung • Rücksacktourist/in • über

10 The right words

Choose the correct words from the box to complete these sentences.
Not all the words are needed.

agent · attendant · backpacker · blue · break · comment · company · create · difficulty · dominant · exam · farm · foreign · gap · hike · itinerary · issue · made · paraphrase · ranked · slow · sort · space · store · technical · via

1 For more news about my travels as a ________ in Australia, watch this ________.

2 I think it's important for people to study ________ languages.

3 My brother spent part of his ________ year working on an organic ________ in Peru.

4 I enjoy visiting other countries, but I wouldn't like to work as a travel ________.

5 My dad can't speak any English but he ________ of ________ himself understood by using body language.

6 In the ________ I didn't copy the ideas we mentioned in class, I wrote a ________.

7 I had great ________ finding a company that could offer me a six-month ________.

8 We made a list of the ________ languages on each continent, ________ by number of speakers.

9 I read the ________ information about the limits of how much you can ________ on the camera.

10 She asked us to ________ on the different ways to ________ a positive impression.

11 Words and phrases ➔ (p. 83)

1 Put the bag under the seat in front of you or in the ____________ __________. ____________________

2 My parents sometimes relax with a _______ in the garden at the weekend. ____________________

3 Good evening, I'd like to ________ a table for four people for 7 pm tomorrow. ____________________

4 In big cities, the _________ is quicker than walking or taking a bus. ____________________

5 I'm at home this afternoon. ________ ____ later for a cup of tea if you want. ____________________

6 She didn't know but didn't say anything. Instead, she just ____________. ____________________

7 When I realized how funny the cartoon was, I ________ _____ ___________. ____________________

8 Why don't you want to go? There are _________ ____ reasons to go. ____________________

9 There is a big _____________ when Mum's ill: Dad has to cook. ____________________

Bier • Gepäckfach • in schallendes Gelächter ausbrechen • Kehrseite • mit den Achseln zucken • reichlich • reserviere • U-Bahn • vorbeikommen

12 Almost the same

Match the sentences with similar meanings.

1 We went by metro.
2 The film doesn't start for an hour.
3 I don't think we need to book.
4 He just shrugged his shoulders when we asked.
5 He came by our house last week.
6 There isn't enough room for everything.
7 It's not a very common name.
8 What he said was really funny.
9 We cycle everywhere.
10 They left a couple of suitcases with us.
11 We had no difficulty finding the address.
12 We were so surprised.

a It's sort of unusual.
b He couldn't tell us the answer.
c We looked after their luggage for a while.
d We need more space for our things.
e We took the Underground.
f It wasn't a problem at all.
g We all burst out laughing.
h It was completely out of the blue.
i We've got plenty of time.
j He visited us when he was passing.
k We can just go. They'll have a table.
l We always go by bike.

13 The right little word

Circle the correct word to complete the sentences.

1 The problem with the photos is that it is out **from • of • in** focus.

2 They were in the area so they just came **past • up • by** and had a chat.

3 The film was so funny I burst **out • off • up** laughing more than once.

4 There are plenty **from • to • of** things to do in the city at night.

5 The train leaves **to • for • at** the airport in twenty minutes.

6 My parents found it hard to make **them • they • themselves** understood.

7 He says he's direct, but he comes **across • by • through** as rude.

8 It was after midnight **at • by • after** the time I had finished the work.

9 He arrived at our home completely **from • out • after** of the blue.

10 This part of the road is dangerous so slow **away • under • down** a little.

14 Scrambled story

Put the parts in the correct order. The first one has been done for you.

a Good morning, everyone. I'm going to talk to you about this photo, which I took while

b backpackers. If you look closely you'll see from her expression she looks sort

c the time I had my camera ready, but I was lucky. The background is a little out of

d wanted is that nature is beautiful, but also dangerous. I hope that comes

e is originally from Italy. She had come via Australia, where she did an internship as

f I was in New Zealand on my gap year. It shows a friend of mine on a beach

g of surprised. The reason is that while we were looking at the sea, out of the

h across here. The day after this, Ana left for home and I went to work on an organic farm.

i blue, some sharks swam by. I was worried that they would have gone by

j a travel agent in an international company. That's her in the foreground, and behind

l her on the left are the mountains that we both hiked through on a one-week trip as

k in the summer. Her name is Ana, and she's a student from Brazil, but her family

m focus, but you can just see them here. So, this is more than a portrait. The message I

Answer: a ☐ ☐ ☐ ☐ ☐ ☐ ☐ ☐ ☐ ☐ ☐ ☐

15 Missing!

Add the missing part of the words.

1 It was difficult to carry my ______________**cases** because they were so heavy.

2 New Zealand is a great place. The only ______________**side** is that it is so far away.

3 On ______________**ic** farms, everything is as natural as possible.

4 These aren't her original words. The text is a ______________**phrase**.

5 My family is Australian, but we are ______________**ally** from Scotland.

6 English is important because it's the ______________**ant** language in so many different areas.

7 If you're looking for ______________**ion**, there are some hotels in the next street.

8 The film was great. It **con**______________ plenty of surprises that you'll love.

9 Many young people leave for the city because of the ______________**y** of finding work in small towns.

10 The flight attendant helped the old man put his bag in the **over**______________ locker.

11 I spent my gap year as a **back**______________ and visited many places in Australia and New Zealand.

12 I applied for a **scholar**______________ but unfortunately the school didn't give me one.

16 The right word

Circle the correct word to complete the sentences.

1 Lots of people don't like reading **technique** • **technical** • **technology** information.

2 What he said was so funny I burst out **laughed** • **laughter** • **laughing** .

3 You should put your baggage in the overhead **locking** • **locker** • **locks** .

4 Each country has its own **customs** • **customers** • **custom** for greeting new people.

5 The hotel restaurant and bar are also open to **non-** • **not** • **no** residents.

6 The article I wrote is going to be in the next **issue** • **event** • **version** of the magazine.

7 Flight **attenders** • **attendance** • **attendants** have to smile and be friendly at all times.

8 All the top **ranked** • **based** • **contained** universities attract lots of foreign students.

9 I want you to have cleaned your room by the **moment** • **hour** • **time** I get back tonight.

10 My American cousin is going to Florida for the spring **breaker** • **break** • **breaking** .

11 Countries use **navigation** • **aviation** • **diplomacy** to solve international problems.

17 Crossword

Across →

2 a plan for a journey that goes via different places
4 an extensive view of a city
6 people who live in one country and travel to another
8 a big test
10 a picture or photo of a person
11 another word for disadvantage
12 communicating with your shoulders
17 what students receive so they don't pay to study
19 car – drive, bike – …
20 a space between two things
21 finding your way from one place to another
22 the underground

Down ↓

1 a simple tourist
3 say in a different way
5 films without the voices of the original actors
7 short periods of work, often for no money
9 the place where you live
13 the art of international understanding
14 when you go for a long walk, often in the country
15 most important or powerful
16 the US word for "luggage"
18 where you put your clothes before a holiday
19 accepted national traditions for things like eating
23 order things

Who are you?

1 Words and phrases ➜ (pp. 10–11)

1 My twin sisters are a bit older than me, in their late ________. ________________

2 One wears her hair in Jamaican ________________; the other has ________ hair. ________________

3 My mum has ________ hair and ___ often ____________ formally. ________________

4 Dad is usually dressed more ____________, maybe in a ________ with jeans. ________________

5 Mum would never wear jeans or anything else made of ________. ________________

6 I was painting and got ________ in my hair. I should wear a ______________. ________________

7 To look really formal, men often wear a _____ around their neck. ________________

8 _________ many young people, I don't like music. ________________

9 If you want to appear ________________, wear dark colours. ________________

10 I love my country. I'm very ______________. ________________

11 His ____________ and beard ____________ that he is a hipster. ________________

12 She was ________________ for a moment, then gave her answer. ________________

13 Older people are often more ________________ than teenagers. ________________

14 Her books are so creative. She has many ____________ ideas. ________________

15 I'd __________ you ____ use this photo, not the other. ________________

angezogen sein • auf etwas hindeuten • Farbe • Frisur • geheimnisvoll • gekräuselt • im Gegensatz zu • Jeansstoff • konservativ • Kopftuch • Krawatte • leger • lockig • nachdenklich • originell • Rasta-Locken • Sakko • Teenageralter • vaterlandsliebend • vorziehen

2 Scrambled sentences

Match the two parts of these sentences.

1 He spent a long time in thoughtful silence
2 He was dressed casually in a blazer
3 I don't think I'll get married in my teens,
4 I wouldn't say his hair is kinky,
5 I've had many different hairstyles
6 My cousin is very conservative,
7 You can smoke outside

a but didn't say anything original.
b but I'd prefer you not to.
c but it's definitely curly.
d but never dreadlocks.
e but not patriotic, surprisingly.
f but without a tie.
g unlike my parents.

3 Words and phrases ➔ *(pp. 12–13)*

1 Last week a ______ came to school to read some of her poems to us.	______
2 I can't ______ a life with a boring ______ every day.	______
3 He talked optimistically about his hopes and ______.	______
4 It was ______ clear that he was very, very wrong.	______
5 I can't ______ with the ______ ringing at 6 am.	______
6 She saw me, ______ ______ me and took her ______ off her head.	______
7 He didn't want to talk, so he ______ them by putting his ______ up.	______
8 The yoga ______ gave some ______ and easy instructions.	______
9 Sorry, the nearest ______ of that shop is in London.	______
10 My grandfather loves music. He has hundreds of old ______.	______
11 Our teacher wants us to do well, so he ______ us work hard.	______
12 We live close to the airport and ______ it's quiet here.	______
13 I can't come tomorrow. ______ ______ I want to, actually.	______
14 This is a ______ unusual word. It isn't used very often.	______

Ausbilder/in • dennoch • Dichter/in • etwas • Kapuze • Kopfhörer • nicht beachten • Routine • Schallplatte • schmerzlich • sich vorstellen • und ich auch nicht • unkompliziert • Wecker • Wunsch • zurechtkommen • Zweigstelle • zwinkern

4 Just the opposite

Complete the sentence with the right opposite.

1 I've never done this before. It's just not part of my ______.

2 Don't listen to what she says. Just try to ______ it.

3 It's not difficult, in fact it's really ______.

4 I was worried about how to manage all the work we have to do, but I can ______.

5 This band isn't different. They just copy others. Their music isn't at all ______.

6 Optimists don't talk about fears and worries; they talk about their hopes and ______.

7 My dad loves history and so does Mum. My sister doesn't, and ______ do I.

8 She looks young so I thought she was a new learner, but in fact she's the ______.

5 Words and phrases ➔ (pp. 14–15)

1 The police don't know the ____________ of the person who attacked the woman. ____________

2 People think differently: they all have a different ____________ on things. ____________

3 Since ________ 2010 this has been ____________: everybody knows it. ____________

4 I'm sure this fantastic film will ________ ____ many people. ____________

5 The way you write ____________ how you think. ____________

6 Poets use ____________ of different ________. ____________

7 ____________ and ____________ are different ways of using pictures in writing. ____________

8 Both are ____________ that compare two different things. ____________

9 He's tall and looks angry, but he's really ____________. ____________

10 The ________ is a bird that is the symbol of peace. ____________

11 This area is ____________ the best and most interesting for young people. ____________

12 Before you write, ____________ how you want the reader to react. ____________

13 ________ are birds that hunt during the day; ________ at night. ____________

ansprechen • Art • berücksichtigen • betrachtet • bildhafte Sprache • Blickwinkel • Eule • Habicht • Identität • Metapher • Mittel • offensichtlich • sanftmütig • Taube • Vergleich • widerspiegeln • zirka

6 Three into one

Match the three parts to make sentences.

1 He went to the library to study local	a owls	k to talk about peace and love.
2 People of all different	b hawks	l about whether this is true.
3 At night you can hear the	c doves	m as your parents.
4 The poet used the imagery of	d genes	n and find out about his family.
5 We have over a hundred	e doubts	o all over the country.
6 Your opinion is just one of many	f devices	p in the woods.
7 He said the soldiers are like	g types	q who hunt and kill.
8 There are serious	h branches	r on the table.
9 You've got the same	i perspectives	s work in the company.
10 He put all his electronic	j records	t on the issue.

7 Words and phrases ➜ (p. 16)

1 This photo shows the earth from ________. ________

2 Young children are ________ by what they see and hear. ________

3 One thing that most people ________ is friendship. ________

4 She looks ________ but she doesn't actually like sport. ________

5 I don't care if my friends are ________ or ________. ________

6 I'm not ________, but I am ________ and want to do well. ________

7 I think it's important to be ________ so that friends can count on you. ________

8 She's very ________. She's ________ about opera. ________

9 I have a ________ and ________ background. ________

10 Barack Obama was the first ________ president of the USA. ________

11 My ________ with my parents taught me to value art and music. ________

12 I like his ________, although it's ________ difficult to understand. ________

13 An adjective or adverb helps you to ________ a statement. ________

14 I think the way you expressed this is quite ________. Make it stronger. ________

15 Use a ________ ________ on the internet to find more information. ________

Afroamerikaner/in • aggressiv • beeinflussen • besonders • Dialekt • ehrgeizig • Erziehung • hetero • konventionell • leidenschaftlich • liberal • musikalisch • näher bestimmen • schätzen • schwach • schwul, lesbisch • sportlich • Suchmaschine • Weltraum • zuverlässig

8 Wrong!

Correct the mistakes. One sentence is correct.

1 I think I'd like to work as a fitness instructer. ________

2 Their relationship was a very passionnate one. ________

3 It's a small country, but it has many different dialekts. ________

4 "As quiet as a mouse" is a simile, not a metapher. ________

5 He's extremely atheletic, but not at all aggressive. ________

6 I used the search engine to find out more about space. ________

7 It's obvous that they didn't have a conventional upbringing. ________

8 Are you sure the information you found is relyable. ________

9 I've got both strait and gay friends who are musical. ________

9 Words and phrases ➜ *(pp. 17–18)*

1 You have to know the ______ rules before you start. ______

2 You should ______ a text for the best ______ effect. ______

3 Tidy your room and put everything in its ______ place. ______

4 Have a good, wide ______ and ______ each paragraph. ______

5 This picture is too small ___ ______ ___ the text. ______

6 The ______ is small and there are too many ______. ______

7 Use ______ ______ to stress words. It adds ______ to your text. ______

8 His writing is ______ and in places not even ______. ______

9 Try a 12 ______ font, and use the spelling ______ to find mistakes. ______

10 To ______ faster on a computer, use all your fingers! ______

11 My ______ ______ is on ______ differences in men and women. ______

12 We need to ______ that there are big differences. ______

13 Boys ______ ___ 40 % of our class but create 80 % of the noise. ______

14 Don't waste time with ______ problems. ______

15 Of course, men and women ______. The biggest difference is ______. ______

16 But ______ ___ ______ ___ pay, there should be no difference. ______

anerkennen • angemessen • biologisch • einrücken • etwas bilden • Fettdruck • formatieren • Funktion • Grund- • im Verhältnis zu • Klarheit • Kursivschrift • lesbar • Meinungsartikel • nicht vorhanden • optisch • Punkt • Rand • Schriftart • sich unterscheiden • tippen • unordentlich • was … betrifft

10 The right word

Choose the correct words from the box to complete these sentences.
Not all the words are needed.

aggressive • Americans • basic • biologically • clarity • differ • font • gender • gentle • legible • indent • influence • opinion • reliable • search • typed • up upbringing • visual • when

1 African ______ make ______ a large percentage of the population in the city.

2 He's normally very ______, but ______ it comes to sport, he can be very ______.

3 To find ideas for his ______ piece, he ______ some key words into the ______ engine.

4 The ______ size is fine, but you should ______ the paragraphs for a better ______ effect.

5 Of course ______ can ______ how you think, and so can your ______.

6 The ______ ways men and women ______ include ______, but also in how they think.

11 Words and phrases → (p. 18)

1 The club has a good ____________ of all age groups. ____________
2 When I was finished, I ____ a friend check my text for mistakes. ____________
3 Things have only ________ improved. They were still bad last year. ____________
4 The party starts at 7 pm, but you can ______ ____ when you want. ____________
5 The __________ gave me __________ advice. It was so stupid! ____________
6 You have made a great ____________ to the project. Thank you. ____________
7 He spent the _______ year in Africa, from January 1 to December 31. ____________
8 Restaurants are big business. ______ ____, everyone needs to eat. ____________
9 We're __________ learning new things about space. ____________
10 You can't completely ________ all danger from life. ____________
11 The film starts later. ___ ____ ________ let's eat. ____________
12 This is a matter of great ____________. It is relevant to us all. ____________

auftauchen • Bedeutung • Beitrag • Berater/in • beseitigen • doch • ganze(r, s) • inzwischen • lächerlich • ständig • veranlassen • Vertretung • vor Kurzem

12 Almost the same

Match the sentences with similar meanings.

1 I didn't do it myself.
2 The film was completely ridiculous.
3 Yesterday was a complete waste of time.
4 We couldn't have done it without you.
5 In this job, being reliable is really important.
6 I know the situation is constantly changing.
7 I guess you could say I'm a sort of counsellor.
8 I showed up quite late.
9 The ideas in the opinion piece were hard to follow.
10 I'm quite new to this company.

a Your contribution was very important.
b I've only recently started here.
c I found it impossible to believe.
d I got there after most people had left.
e I spent the entire day waiting for them.
f I had someone do it for me.
g I recognize that it never stays the same.
h I didn't think there was enough clarity.
i I think it's impossible to value it too highly.
j I listen to people and give them advice.

13 Words and phrases ➜ (p. 19)

1 Every unit in this book has a different ________. Unit 1 is about identity. ________

2 We're going to ________ and try to understand the imagery of the poem. ________

3 I ________ some good news yesterday. I'm going to be an uncle! ________

4 There are two ________: do we stay or go? ________

5 It was the ________ of the article that ________ my ________. ________

6 She ________ our ________ ________ a very important question. ________

7 It's a very ________ article. The author wants to annoy his readers. ________

8 We're looking for a ________ ________ the problem. ________

9 You should use facts and examples to ________ ________ your opinions. ________

10 In case you've forgotten what I said, I'll ________ the facts. ________

11 The situation ________ ________ a new approach. ________

12 In the past, the ________ were divided in many schools. ________

13 I'm too young to think about ________. I also don't have a girlfriend. ________

14 You need a ________ ________ between these ideas in your report. ________

Absatzumbruch • auf etwas aufmerksam machen • Aufmerksamkeit • Ehe • erhalten • Geschlecht • Lösung • Möglichkeit • noch einmal formulieren • provozierend • Schlagzeile, Überschrift • Schwerpunkt • untermauern • untersuchen • verlangen

14 Missing words

Add missing words to two of the four gaps in each sentence.

1 When ________ comes to ________ business, ________ new problems call ________ new solutions.

2 I wasn't wearing ________ a suit, and nor ________ my friend, but ________ everyone else ________ dressed in blazers.

3 I'd prefer ________ to go out ________ tonight; after ________, we've been out ________ the last three nights.

4 To make ________ people ________ attention to your writing ________ use bold ________ and attractive photos.

5 His ________ arms are very long ________ relation ________ his body, but he ________ still looks very athletic.

6 Say something new instead of restating ________ facts, ________ and ________ someone check ________ your spelling.

7 I'm looking for ________ examples to back ________ the main points, as ________ that ________ considered important.

8 Tomorrow's ________ important, so ________ the meantime relax, ________ though that doesn't appeal ________ you.

15 Words and phrases ➜ (pp. 20–21)

1 I've got a __________ idea of the topic but don't understand all the details. __________

2 I know how much you earn: we talk openly about _____ in this __________. __________

3 It's illegal to __________ __________ foreigners. __________

4 _______, my parents work too much and never _______ any _______ _____. __________

5 Don't _______ your _______. I can understand you better if you speak quietly. __________

6 You can get a ______ of €100 if you do that. Somebody might call the police. __________

7 We _______ the problem of __________ pay for women very __________. __________

8 It didn't take a lot of __________ until he agreed. __________

9 At first I didn't want to go, but she __________ me that it would be fun. __________

10 __________ are fun little stories but not as useful as __________ examples. __________

11 Your story is great. It's really creative and very __________. __________

12 __________ questions don't really need answers, do they? __________

13 You wrote this. You can't _______ it. I recognize your style. __________

14 "Great" is more __________ than "good". __________

allgemein • Anekdote • Arbeitsplatz • ausdrucksstark • bestreiten • Bezahlung • diskriminieren • ernst nehmen • Geldstrafe • leider • nachdrücklich • rhetorisch • sachlich • seine Stimme erheben • sich frei nehmen • überreden • Überredung • ungleich

16 Missing parts

Add the missing part of the words.

1 I didn't really expect an answer. My question was ____________________**al**.

2 The players were in no doubt about how the crowd felt. They were very ____________________**ive**!

3 We won 8:0. It was a very ____________________**ic** victory.

4 I had to use a lot of ____________________**ion** to make him change his mind about our party.

5 Some companies still ____________________**ate** against women by paying them less than men.

6 Climate change and pollution are things we take very ____________________**ly**.

7 Their music is very ____________________**cative**: they want to make you react strongly.

8 Please stop doing that and pay ____________________**ion** to what I'm saying.

9 One thing that makes the text a little boring is that it is so ____________________**ual**. Too many statistics.

10 You can either do it today or tomorrow. Those are the only two ____________________**ions**.

17 Words and phrases ➔ (p. 22)

1 I know that Maurice is French, but ________ that not much. ________
2 We're learning about animal ______ this week in biology. ________
3 The twins have the same ________ but are ____________ people. ________
4 The future of the ________ ______ depends on us, the young. ________
5 I cannot imagine life without ____________. ________
6 I find ________ history really interesting. The Greeks are my favourite. ________
7 After the accident, the car was left in the field and ________ away. ________
8 Over the years, the cliff has been ________ by the sea. ________
9 You can't ________ history ____ a few dates. You need the whole picture. ________
10 There's been another ____________ in Japan. ________
11 This is a rare ________ of bird. It can only be found in this area. ________
12 This was the wettest summer since __________ began in 1871. ________
13 Plants ______ ________ before humans. And they will be after humans too. ________
14 They found the __________ of ten people when they built the car park. ________

abtragen • Art • Aufzeichnung • da sein • einzeln • Erdbeben • Gen • Menschheit • reduzieren • Skelett • Technologie • über … hinaus • uralt • verrosten • Zelle

18 The right word

Circle the correct word to complete the sentences.

1 Dad got a **fine • found • find** for parking in the wrong place.
2 Nuclear war could be the end of the human **type • race • life** .
3 I know the capital city, but **above • beyond • over** that, not much.
4 It was so loud we had to **lift • rise • raise** our voices to be heard.
5 Dinosaurs haven't been **along • about • around** for a long time.
6 Many buildings were damaged in the earth **tremble • quake • movement** .
7 I need to take a couple of days **out • away • off** to go to see my grandparents.
8 You can't **refuse • deny • persuade** that this actually happened.
9 It's not easy to cope when you have a job with low **pay • paid • paying** .
10 It would be great, but I don't think it will happen, **sad • sadness • sadly** .

19 Words and phrases ➜ (pp. 22–25)

1 She didn't believe me and just looked at me in ________________.	________________
2 The news that Justin was getting married created a lot of ______________.	________________
3 Life is full of _____ _____ ________. There are always good days and bad days.	________________
4 I'll test your __________________ of the text: how well do you understand it?	________________
5 Without this ________ _____ from the Baltic, we can't watch TV.	________________
6 The car needs a lot of work. The _________ to it will take two weeks.	________________
7 It's dangerous to go sailing in rain or _____ ________.	________________
8 They hope to ___________ the work by the weekend. Then they can relax.	________________
9 They planted some trees in the back ______ of their house in Texas.	________________
10 When he finished speaking, no one cheered, but there was polite ___________.	________________
11 The ________ of the film was really exciting and unexpected.	________________
12 Not a _______ kid liked the _________________ for the new game.	________________

abschließen • Aufregung • Beifall • einzige(r, s) • Erstaunen • Garten • Höhen und Tiefen • Höhepunkt • Reparatur • starker Wind • Überlandleitung • Verständnis • Werbespot

20 More about writing

Put the parts in the correct order.
The first one has been done for you.

a If you are writing an opinion piece – or any other text at

b want to continue reading your text. It's obvious, after

c anecdotes; your ideas may be original, conventional or even

d all, in fact – it's worth remembering that the key to

e grammar or spelling mistakes. The thing you must not ignore

f who is reading it. So let me give you an important piece of

g understood or checking your work to see you avoid making

h aggressive; you can use a style that is totally factual or simply

i success is much more than simply making yourself

j the importance of this basic fact, you can write any way

k you like. It doesn't matter if you decide to be provocative or

l all, that the reader has the option of stopping reading

m is that your text must appeal in some way to the person

n ridiculous, but what the reader really values when it comes

o whenever he or she feels bored. As long as you recognise

p advice. Your first job as a writer is to make the reader

q to reading any text is that it must be interesting.

Answer: a ☐ ☐ ☐ ☐ ☐ ☐ ☐ ☐ ☐ ☐ ☐ ☐ ☐ ☐ ☐ ☐

2 Unit • Volume 6

What makes a community?

1 Words and phrases → (pp. 30–32)

1 My dad was happy when he got a ____ ____ of €200 per month.

2 Prices often ____ faster than the money we earn.

3 That wasn't what I'd ____ a successful ____.

4 There was a story about a people who lived in the Amazonian ____.

5 The ____ here in Malta are all very friendly.

6 When we got to the village, the ____ just stood and ____ us.

7 Drinking beer ____ people's ____: they can get very loud.

8 He got ____ with his ____ at the wedding. It wasn't funny.

9 There isn't much gold in the ground. ____ it is expensive.

10 To avoid the cut getting ____, you should put ____ on it.

11 It's hot today, so make sure you drink lots of ____.

12 In the afternoon we ____ slowly around the village.

13 Good ____ are important, ____ ____ how young you are.

beobachten • Besprechung • betrunken • charakterisieren • daher • die Einheimischen • Dorfbewohner/in • Dschungel • entzündet • Flüssigkeit • ganz gleich • Gehaltserhöhung • Manieren • Salbe • schlendern • sich auswirken auf • steigen • Verhalten • Verwandte(r)

2 Scrambled sentences

Match the two parts of these sentences.

1 She has done some great work, so she has hopes
2 There are still tribes who have never been out
3 She didn't know the way, so she stopped and asked one
4 It was a complete waste of time, so she walked out
5 Every month there is a meeting
6 It might surprise you, but the human body is largely made
7 Spitting in public is another example
8 She's got the curly hair and fair skin
9 She had a crash and ruined the car, which is a result

a of the meeting.
b of all the villagers.
c of all her relatives.
d of getting a pay rise.
e of her bad behaviour.
f of being drunk at the time.
g of the locals.
h of liquid.
i of the jungle.

3 Words and phrases ➜ (p. 33)

1 When Dad was in town, he ___ ___ see an old school-friend. ___

2 My sister is so annoying. She does bad things to me ___ ___. ___

3 He was so rude. I've decided to ___ him a ___. ___

4 They ___ gold for ___. ___

5 It's not ___ to use "Hi, babe!" as a ___ to a stranger. ___

6 His email was so rude! I'm just deciding how to ___. ___

7 The fence ___ are there to protect the ___ in the water. ___

8 I bumped into my teacher in town ___ ___ ___. ___

9 If you had any ___, you wouldn't do things like that. ___

10 He fixed a kind of flag to the ___ in his garden. ___

11 The two enemies finally ___ ___ ___ ___. ___

12 He's got lots of money, but he's quite ___. ___

13 She always wears ___ in the summer, but never ___ ___. ___

14 You should go to the gym more. Look at your fat ___! ___

angemessen • Bauch • Begrüßung • eine Lektion erteilen • knauserig, geizig • Kugel • mit Absicht • neulich • Pfahl • Pfosten • reagieren • Sandale • sich einigen • Stöckelschuhe • Vernunft • Wasserschildkröte • zufälligerweise

4 Just the opposite

Complete the sentence with the right opposite.

1 I wouldn't say he's generous. In fact, he's the opposite. He's ___.

2 It was a genuine mistake, I promise. I didn't do it ___.

3 I didn't say I'm meeting her next week. I said I saw her ___.

4 I didn't start the argument. He was rude and aggressive. I just ___.

5 I didn't rush into town. I had plenty of time so I just ___ there.

6 Prices of some foods have fallen, but not fruit. That has ___ a lot.

7 Flat shoes like ___ are so much more comfortable than high heels.

8 That's not a picture of his back! It's his ___!

9 He wanted one thing, I wanted another, but eventually we ___.

10 I spend much more time with my friends than with my ___.

5 Words and phrases ➜ (pp. 34–37)

1 My little brother was ill, so Mum stayed at home to ______ ______ him. ______________

2 Different people have different religious __________. It's normal. ______________

3 He sometimes hides ________ under the ____________ to eat when he's in bed. ______________

4 She __________ _____ her birthday present and started to __________ it. ______________

5 He _____________ with his eyes that someone was behind the door. ______________

6 You ___________ her when you said that her feet were ________. ______________

7 The marks on the wall measure the _________ of the children. ______________

8 The teacher said something funny that made them ________. ______________

9 To make a hole for the post, we're going to need a ________. ______________

10 I laughed so much, but you sat there ______ ___ __________ ______. ______________

11 He asked us for our __________ of the situation. ______________

12 I went to buy milk, ________ ______, butter, ______ ____ ____. ______________

13 We spent our holidays in Warnemünde, on the ________ _____. ______________

14 I ________ the bottle in the air and tried to ________ the waiter's _____. ______________

15 The _______ at Dad's office are all ________________ about sport. ______________

(an-, hoch)heben • auspacken • Auswertung • begeistert • Belegschaft • beleidigen • Blickkontakt herstellen • Brötchen • deuten • Glaube • greifen nach • kichern • Matratze • ohne eine Miene zu verziehen • Ostsee • Schaufel • sich kümmern um • Süßigkeiten • übelriechend • und so weiter • Wachstum

6 Three into one

Match the three parts to make sentences.

1 It was the headline that	a came	k something was wrong.
2 It was cold, but she was sweating, which	b traded	l her eye first.
3 She got home and immediately	c lifted	m when she first heard it.
4 It was an unusual name, and she	d reached	n for abandoned children.
5 In the film they	e giggled	o to an understanding about it.
6 She wanted to change channels so she	f indicated	p for the remote control.
7 The two sides finally	g caught	q gold for bullets.
8 She started an organisation that	h insulted	r the parcel.
9 She found a secret hiding place when she	i unwrapped	s up the table.
10 She lost her job the second time she	j cared	t her boss

7 Words and phrases ➜ *(pp. 37–40)*

1 The present was ______________ – I just couldn't believe it.	______________
2 He works as a _______ ____________ and he's a keen _________ too.	______________
3 Is it OK to drink the _____ ________ here?	______________
4 My mistake was so stupid that I felt ______________.	______________
5 I'm learning how to play the ________ after school.	______________
6 We want to add some _____________ to the ___________ we filmed today.	______________
7 After some ______________, my brother has decided to leave school.	______________
8 I want to see the new James Bond film. The __________ are very positive.	______________
9 The teacher asked us to _________ a ____________ restaurant.	______________
10 I read a lot of __________; it's ______ ____ interesting as factual books.	______________
11 The problem was a result of a ________________________.	______________
12 They asked me to __________ the scene of a mother __________ her child.	______________
13 There's a difference between being stupid and being ____________.	______________
14 I can't come today. Can we _____ it _____, at least _____ _____?	______________
15 The poor dog was ______________ at the side of the road.	______________

aufschieben • ausgesetzt • baden • Bankangestellte(r) • Betrachtung • erfunden • erzählen • Erzählung • Film(material) • Geige • genauso • Leitungswasser • Missverständnis • Prosaliteratur • Radfahrer/in • rezensieren • Rezension • unglaublich • unwissend • verlegen • vorerst

8 Almost the same

Match the two sentences with similar meanings.

1 I had an absolutely amazing time.
2 My face went the colour of a tomato!
3 The room looked like everyone had left in a hurry.
4 This is just a temporary solution.
5 They came on Tuesday, not Thursday.
6 He works as a bank assistant.
7 This is his opinion of the latest film.
8 What he said shows he knows nothing about it.
9 The meeting will take place later in the month.
10 This isn't a true story, you know.

a It was a misunderstanding.
b It was abandoned.
c It's a review.
d It's been put off for a while.
e It was just incredible
f It was an ignorant comment.
g It's fiction.
h It's his job.
i It was so embarrassing
j It'll do for now.

9 Words and phrases ➔ (pp. 40–41)

1 Some people are against ____________ in public. ____________
2 I had to explain it several times before he ____________ understood. ____________
3 It was so cold that my fingers were ____________ blue. ____________
4 As it got dark, the jungle ________ louder and louder. ____________
5 That's not just big, it's ____________! ____________
6 The visit to the museum was very ____________. We learned a lot. ____________
7 We're ____________ opposed to building more roads here. ____________
8 She's very popular. She has an ____________ smile and is very clever. ____________
9 I am sorry to ____________ you that your application for the job was unsuccessful. ____________
10 I liked the film's special effects, but the ________ was ridiculous. ____________
11 He stared at his empty cup to ________ that he wanted another cup of coffee. ____________
12 I could ____________ the book in one word: brilliant! ____________
13 Good: the ____________ that you wrote ____________ most of the key points. ____________
14 Mum has been learning French for years, but her level is still not ____________. ____________
15 It's very cold in the mountains, so be sure to take ____________ clothes. ____________

abdecken • anbauen • andeuten • buchstäblich • entschieden • fesselnd • fortgeschritten • geeignet • Handlung • informieren • lehrreich • riesig • schließlich • Stillen • werden • zusammenfassen • Zusammenfassung

10 The right word

Choose the correct words from the box to complete these sentences. Not all the words are needed.

advanced • breastfeeding • engaging • enormous • eventually • grow • incredible • informative • insulted • listening • literally • plot • strongly • suitable • summary • violin • when

1 When I said he was a monster I didn't mean it ____________, but I accept that he felt ____________.
2 When you write a ____________, it's important to be ____________.
3 I'm not sure the subject of the film is ____________ for children. The ____________ is also difficult to follow.
4 I signed up for a ____________ course at ____________ level, and it was very effective.
5 People felt so ____________ about ____________ that they went on a demonstration.
6 The number of people who follow her blog is ____________ because the style is really ____________.
7 The first time I tried to ____________ vegetables was a disaster, but I ____________ got it right.
8 It's ____________ how many people have taken up the ____________ at school.

11 Words and phrases ➜ (pp. 42–43)

1 I'm not tall enough to paint the ceiling. I need a ________.	________
2 I love films and novels of all ________ – except horror.	________
3 His latest novel is ______-____________________, and it's very funny.	________
4 The ________ actually happened in Bonn, but the film ___ _____ in Berlin.	________
5 The film makes ____________ use of humour. It's ____________.	________
6 Her new book is __________. It's the sad __________ of the life of a refugee.	________
7 I don't like films that put a lot of ____________ on politics.	________
8 The article ______________ the problems of young people in society today.	________
9 This book was recommended ________, and I find it very ___________.	________
10 If you want an ________________ book for your holiday, this is a great ______.	________
11 Our visit to the art gallery was very ____________. We all had fun.	________
12 Some modern portraits aren't very __________.	________
13 The plot is very exciting: I found the book really ___________.	________
14 Her last film was a very ______________ statement about life and love.	________
15 I try to _______ having long meetings on a Friday afternoon.	________

aussagekräftig • äußerst • autobiografisch • Betonung • bewegend • fesselnd • Gattung • halb- • hervorheben • lebensecht • Leiter • Lektüre • lesenswert • Schilderung • spielen in • unheimlich witzig • unterhaltsam • unterhaltsam • Verbrechen • vermeiden • wirkungsvoll

12 That's wrong!

Circle and correct two mistakes in each line. One line is correct.

1 The film was semi-autobiographic, but it was hillarious. ________ ________

2 Her account emphazizes family problems. It's not an easy reading. ________ ________

3 The director sat the film in London in the 1970s. I found it totally griping. ________ ________

4 The government said nothing meaningful about how to combat crime effectively. ________ ________

5 When I first saw it, I couldn't beleive it was a model. It was so livelike. ________ ________

6 The author wrote many very entertained books in different genre. ________ ________

7 This is an informating test on the advantages of brestfeeding. ________ ________

8 I always try to aviod walking under laders: it can cause bad luck. ________ ________

9 Their new house is enorm! It's literaly twice the size of ours. ________ ________

13 Words and phrases ➜ (p. 44)

1 Modern cities have a great ____________ of people living in them. ____________

2 The museum has a great ____________ of clothes worn by famous people. ____________

3 I'm planning to go to a new photography ____________ this weekend. ____________

4 It seems that some countries just can't live in ____________ with one another. ____________

5 Our school tries to ____________ the latest developments in technology. ____________

6 In his blog, he wrote something very ____________ about our teachers. ____________

7 Do you think there is an element of truth in this ____________? ____________

8 Lots of my class are ill. Only five kids were ____________ at school yesterday. ____________

9 This film really ____________ the atmosphere of city life. ____________

10 The writer has just copied and ____________ ideas from the Internet. ____________

11 Our new bathroom is being ____________ tomorrow. ____________

12 We want lots of people to ____________ ____ the demonstration. ____________

abfällig • anwesend • Ausstellung • (ein)fangen • einfügen • einrichten • Harmonie • Klischee(vorstellung) • mit offenen Armen begrüßen • teilnehmen an • Vielfalt • Vorführung

14 Keywords

Rewrite the sentences using the keywords so they mean the same as the original.
Don't change the keyword in any way.

1 There were more than a million signatures on the petition. signed

Over a ____ the petition.

2 My salary has been the same for more than three years. pay

I haven't had ____ least three years ago.

3 I don't care how much it costs, I'm going to buy it. no

I've decided to buy it, ____ expensive it is.

4 He behaves like that deliberately to annoy me. on

He does things like that ____ because he knows it annoys me.

5 The meeting was going to happen tomorrow but we've had to change the date to next Tuesday. off

Tomorrow's meeting has ____ until next Tuesday.

6 He left early because he didn't want to be driving when the traffic was busiest. avoid

The reason he left early was in ____ the worst of the traffic.

15 Words and phrases ➜ (pp. 45–46)

1 I think it's really important to ________ __ ________ ________ racism.	________
2 Life in the ________ is very different from life in smaller cities.	________
3 My cousin spends hours playing ________ reality games.	________
4 Footage of the ________ was ________ on the wall during the talk.	________
5 Mum is going to her first international ________. She's very excited!	________
6 We work for a young and ________ company that is growing quickly.	________
7 There was an ________ silence everywhere in the city centre.	________
8 The ________ of the castle brought back ________ memories of war.	________
9 The ________ makes the atmosphere of the film even more ________.	________
10 Every day there's a different ________ in the news.	________
11 You'll ________ improve your English ____ living in the UK for a year.	________
12 We eat too much these days. We should do more ________ to stay healthy.	________
13 The car stopped because it had run out of ________.	________
14 You're never far from a ______ ________ in the United States.	________
15 The high salary and long holidays make the job sound very ________.	________

Anblick • auf jeden Fall • Benzin • Bewegung • Demonstration • dynamisch • ergreifend • Filmmusik • gespenstisch • Hauptstadt • indem du … • Kongress • Politiker/in • projizieren • Stellung beziehen zu • Tankstelle • unwirklich • verlockend • virtuell

16 Missing!

Add the missing parts of the words.

1 I get a lot of ________**er**________. I never take the bus: I walk everywhere.

2 A lot of people don't trust ________**itic**________. They think they just want power.

3 The plot of the film was ridiculous, but the ________**und**________ was great – lots of reggae.

4 The job sounds quite boring but the salary makes it more ________**ive** than many others.

5 We're taking part in a ________**fer**________ on improving the lives of refugees.

6 After school, lots of young people move to the ________**it**________ to look for work.

7 My favourite band is playing here next year. I'm ________**init**________ going to get a ticket.

8 He said something very ________**rog**________ about this area, which annoyed me.

9 When the lesson is boring, I just don't feel like ________**ici**________.

17 Words and phrases ➜ (p. 47)

1 I don't think you can say that all ___________ issues are important. ___________

2 My ___________ ___ the local sports team keeps me busy at weekends. ___________

3 I first ___ ___________ in the cycling club a couple of years ago. ___________

4 My sister's an ___________. She's always planning her next ___________. ___________

5 My mum ___________ for the local hospital. It was a good ___________. ___________

6 Is there a test for people who want to become German ___________? ___________

7 We're lucky to live in a ___________, where we can vote for our government. ___________

8 The minister is starting a new ___________ to fight unemployment. ___________

9 I felt so strongly about it that I wrote to my ___ and asked her to get involved. ___________

10 The results of the ___________ ___ about traffic pollution are interesting. ___________

11 I'm not a member of any political ___________, nor do I want to be. ___________

12 I'm going to start a ___________ against closing the village library. ___________

13 I don't think the government's ___________ on immigration is working. ___________

Aktivist/in • Anliegen • Beteiligung an • Demokratie • Initiative • Kampagne • Meinungsumfrage • Parlamentsmitglied • Partei • Politik • politisch • sich einsetzen • sich engagieren • (Staats-)Bürger/in • Unterschriftensammlung

18 Scrambled sentences

Put the parts in the correct order.
The first one has been done for you.

b a stand on issues are generally very happy to take part in public opinion

d polls, which is another way of making sure your voice as an active citizen is heard

a You sometimes hear it said that young people are not interested in

f as democracy, pollution and fair treatment for everyone. An enormous number participate

c in demonstrations for causes they believe in, and show their support for

e politics, but that really depends on your definition of politics. It's true

g that few people in their teens join a party, or want to become an

h get involved in campaigns for things they feel strongly about, such

i petitions when they feel strongly about government policies that they disagree

j MP, but involvement takes many forms. Many young people do

l immigrants and victims of racism, for example, and many are happy to sign

k with. Even those school children and students who don't go on marches to take

Answer: a ☐ ☐ ☐ ☐ ☐ ☐ ☐ ☐ ☐ ☐ ☐

19 Words and phrases ➜ *(pp. 47–50)*

1 The ____________ ________ hopes to make the government change its policy. ____________

2 Many people were surprised by the result of the ____________. ____________

3 A speed limit of 20 km/h is one way of improving road ________. ____________

4 My ____________ is very similar to my father's. ____________

5 Over 100,000 people ________ the petition. ____________

6 The workers ____________ safer working conditions and better pay. ____________

7 In the United States, they ______ the president every four years. ____________

8 People ________________ against the government in London yesterday. ____________

9 When you do a presentation, your first ______ should have the title. ____________

10 As time is limited, I'll focus on the most important ________ of the problem. ____________

11 We haven't made a lot of progress, but we are slowly moving ____________. ____________

12 Improving the ________________ of the country will cost billions. ____________

13 Unfortunately, ________ people attended the meeting than I expected. ____________

14 Money is a problem, so the company is trying to keep costs as _____ as possible. ____________

15 My favourite sport in the Olympics is ______________ swimming. ____________

Aspekt • demonstrieren • Folie • fordern, verlangen • Infrastruktur • Lobby • niedrig • Sicherheit • synchronisiert • unterschreiben • Unterschrift • Volksentscheid • voran • wählen • weniger

20 Quiz time!

1 The British put petrol in their cars. What do Americans use? ____________

2 What's the political system where everyone can vote for the government? ____________

3 What's the word for a member of a country? ____________

4 The English are polite, the Italians are noisy. These are … ____________

5 The music accompanying a film is called the … ____________

6 This is a slow, relaxed way of walking. ____________

7 Beer and water are examples of this, but bread and butter are not. ____________

8 A part of your body that rhymes with 'smelly'. ____________

9 A synonym for 'as a result' or 'consequently' ____________

10 This describes a story that is not true. ____________

21 Which verb?

Complete the sentences with the correct form of the verbs.

come • go • keep • make • take

1 I was interested in the situation, so he ______________ me posted.

2 The article I wrote on gender differences ______________ viral.

3 I haven't found a good photo to go with my text, but I'll ______________ looking.

4 Not everyone agreed with equality then. Many people ______________ a different view.

5 It ______________ a big difference when people stood up for their rights.

6 When I was doing research, I ______________ across some interesting statistics.

7 The photos ______________ up a lot of space, so I decided not to use them.

8 I said it was a bad idea, but they still ______________ ahead and did it.

9 It's not always easy to ______________ comparisons between different cultures.

10 After my presentation she ______________ up to me and said it was interesting.

22 Correcting compound nouns

In each line, (circle) a word that doesn't fit.
Then replace it with a word that you have circled in another line.

1 The (high) water is perfectly safe to drink here, and so are the water fountains. tap

2 I thought I could hear the sound of a brass race playing the national anthem in the park. ______________

3 There should be a danger sign warning people not to climb the dairy line.

4 Many people buy holidays online using tap engines so there are fewer travel agents today. ______________

5 The bank assistant asked if there were opinion products in the pumpkin pie. ______________

6 The pressure group leader wrote a good rubbish piece about pollution in the Baltic Sea. ______________

7 "The future of the human break depends on bank assistants", he said with a straight face. ______________

8 On our road trip we threw the bread rolls in the search bin because they were green. ______________

9 Flight attendants generally aren't allowed to wear power heels as a matter of safety. ______________

10 The last lessons in high school before the spring band were on civil rights. ______________

3 Unit · Volume 6

How is the world changing?

1 Words and phrases ➜ (pp. 52–53)

1 I have a ________ on my desk at home, so I know where countries are.	________
2 There has been great ________ ________ in the last ten years.	________
3 The company offer same-day ________ for anything you buy.	________
4 They agreed to ________ the ________ tomorrow afternoon.	________
5 People worry that ________ might create unemployment.	________
6 ________ skills are very important these days.	________
7 I think ________ and ________ will change many traditional jobs.	________
8 I'm not sure about the advantages of ________ intelligence.	________
9 We need ________ to ________ trees and plants.	________
10 I'm allergic to ________ so I couldn't work in ________.	________
11 We know that ________ improves when workers feel motivated.	________
12 Some people say if a job can be done by a ________, it should be.	________
13 I doubt computers can completely ________ people.	________
14 We're having a ________ ________ on new forms of energy.	________

Automatisierung · bestäuben · Biene · Blütenstaub · digital · Drohne · ersetzen · Fortschritt · Gerät · Globus · Herstellung · künstlich · Landwirtschaft · liefern · Lieferung · Paket · Podiumsdiskussion · Roboter · technologisch

2 The right words

Finish the sentences.

1 The company's going to be in trouble unless we can improve
2 With the internet it's easy to find out what is happening across the
3 They brought my new washing machine and asked me to sign for the
4 They left me a note because I was out when they tried to deliver the
5 The article explained the role of insects that pollinate, such as
6 At the end of the conference the main topics were reviewed in a
7 Feeding a growing population makes great demands on our
8 I can imagine that in the future letters will be delivered by
9 For our science project we had to design and build a

a package.
b panel discussion.
c drones.
d delivery.
e production.
f robot.
g globe.
h bees.
i agriculture.

3 Words and phrases ➔ (p. 54)

1 One of the __________ of technology is that it saves us time. __________

2 After a busy week, we'll all __________ from a relaxing weekend. __________

3 It was a ______, but I decided to leave my job and start my own business. __________

4 I couldn't see in the sauna, because it was full of ________. __________

5 Manchester was a centre of the _______ industry, mostly cotton. __________

6 Each new piece of technology is the result of some ____________. __________

7 Are you against using __________ power as a source of ____________? __________

8 The __________ light made a big change to how people lived and worked. __________

9 Science fiction films often present a certain ________ of life in the future. __________

10 We need strict supervision of companies that store ______________ ________. __________

11 I __________ ____ my computer. I can't imagine life without it! __________

12 The police managed to __________ the crowd, but not the noise level. __________

13 Her new poem _______ ______ the death of her mother. __________

14 From her ______ of voice, I knew Mum was ____________ ________ Dad. __________

Abfall • angewiesen sein auf • Atom- • beherrschen • besorgt um • Dampf • elektrisch • handeln von etwas • Neuerung • profitieren • radioaktiv • Risiko • Strom • Ton • Tuch • Vorstellung • Vorteil

4 Scrambled sentences

Match the two parts of the dialogues.

1 It's not what he says that annoys me.
2 Is that smoke coming from the house?
3 Have you always organised results this way?
4 Is that a disadvantage?
5 Are you sure this will work?
6 Do you need this?
7 You're not still using that old machine, are you?
8 It's not dairy products that make you sneeze?
9 Is that a real diamond?
10 Do we still need to arrange the meeting?

a No, it's a benefit.
b No, it's artificial.
c No, it's waste.
d No, it's pollen.
e No, it's a risk.
f No, it's steam.
g No, it's been dealt with.
h No, it's an innovation.
i No, I know. It's the tone.
j No, it's been replaced.

5 Words and phrases ➜ (pp. 55–56)

1 You learn important things by doing sport: team work, ______ ______. ______

2 I don't agree with the way life in the city is ______ in the film. ______

3 The village now has a ______ need for medicine and clean water. ______

4 Our ______ will depend on how we adapt to new challenges. ______

5 Only one team ______ ___ ______ ___ our success in the competition. ______

6 Yesterday, it ______ to rain all day. But it stayed dry. ______

7 Do the advantages of nuclear power ______ the disadvantages? ______

8 I have a ______ memory of seeing them before, but I'm not sure when it was. ______

9 I won't keep you long because I'm ______ of the time. ______

10 This latest discovery could have important ______ in medicine. ______

11 If we don't look after ______, the planet won't ______ long. ______

12 The workers ______ ___ ______ after ______ of bullying by the managers. ______

13 I don't understand the ______ of events that led to this problem. ______

14 The letter "e" has the highest ______ in the English language. ______

15 I didn't mind what he said. It was his ______ that made me sad. ______

abbilden • Abfolge • Art und Weise • bedrohen • bewusst • eine Bedrohung darstellen für • Einsatzmöglichkeit • Fall • halten • Häufigkeit • in den Streik treten • komplex • Natur • Überleben • überwiegen • unbestimmt • verzweifelt • zum Beispiel

6 Three into one

Match the three parts to make sentences.

1 Our resources won't last forever. Our	a manner	k unless conditions improved.
2 I'm very concerned that this	b sequence	l of our orders.
3 My first job was delivering rolls of	c strike	m to shops in the area.
4 This new technology poses no particular	d case	n depends on science.
5 The new system allows us to reduce the	e frequency	o of that to medicine.
6 The employees threatened to go on	f nature	p of approaching things.
7 I like her because of her positive	g application	q have not all worked well.
8 Once we understood the correct	h threat	r hasn't been dealt with yet.
9 Man's various attempts to control	i survival	s things became easier.
10 First we have research, then the	j loth	t to the work we are doing.

7 Words and phrases ➜ (p. 57)

1 An important lesson in life is learning how to ________ your time and money. ________
2 My phone is almost empty. I need to ________ it. ________
3 To see the next photo, you have to ________ the screen of your tablet. ________
4 The ________ in my camera is great. It lasts for ages. ________
5 On the screen you see two ________ on the left and the ________ at the top. ________
6 The first IT lesson taught them about the ________ and the ________ ________. ________
7 It gets confusing if you have too many browser ________ open at the same time. ________
8 This website is clear and simple, which makes it easy to ________. ________
9 The more ________ you have, the more ________ your computer needs. ________
10 After I'd ________ those two programs I decided to ________ them. ________
11 If you can't ________ photos, you won't be able to ________ them either. ________
12 I found some amazing cat films when I was ________ the web last night. ________
13 Can you show me how to ________ the ________ on my laptop? ________
14 ________ can be dangerous, so my email app ________ them. ________
15 I don't accept every ________ ________ I receive. ________

Anhang • anpassen • aufladen • ausführen • Batterie, Akku • Daten • einführen • Einstellungen • Freundschaftsanfrage • Knopf • löschen • Menü • mit etwas umgehen • Reiter • Speicher • sperren • steuern • Suchleiste • surfen • Symbol • wischen

8 Computer issues

Choose the correct words in the correct form from the box to complete these short texts. Not all the words are needed.

attachment • battery • browse • charge • customize • delete • friend • icon • import • manage • menu • request • run • setting • swipe • tab

1 I was **(1)** ________ the internet when I noticed I'd got a **(2)** ________ from someone I didn't know. Normally I **(3)** ________ things like that, and I also never open **(4)** ________ on emails from sources I'm not familiar with.

2 I made a stupid mistake last night. I had a lot of **(5)** ________ open, and I was **(6)** ________ a couple of different programs too. I'd **(7)** ________ to find some great materials I wanted to **(8)** ________ into my presentation, but then my **(9)** ________ was suddenly empty and I lost everything!

3 I clicked on the **(10)** ________ and found how to **(11)** ________ things on the computer, like what size I want the buttons to be. So now, the **(12)** ________ are all my own!

9 Words and phrases → (p. 58)

1 He was annoying me so I told him to ______ ______.	______
2 There's an interesting ______ ______ on bees in the newspaper.	______
3 The bear was caught in a ______, which had injured its foot.	______
4 Bees don't normally ______, but it's painful when they do.	______
5 Last year the ______ was bad. The bad weather killed most of the ______.	______
6 There are several ______ we have to consider when analysing the problem.	______
7 Our ______ of ______ has had a negative influence on many insects.	______
8 A ______ diet is difficult if only a limited ______ of food is available.	______
9 ______ often ______ the animals they live in.	______
10 The illness weakened his ______ ______, so he is ______ ______ viruses.	______
11 ______ is one way of fighting the cold.	______
12 ______ ______, living in large colonies helps.	______

abschwirren • abwechslungsreich • anfällig für etwas • Außerdem … • Auswahl • Ernte • Faktor • Falle • Feldfrucht • Immunsystem • Parasit • Schädlingsbekämpfungsmittel • schwächen • Sonderbericht • stechen • Verwendung • Winterschlaf

10 Almost the same

Match the two sentences with similar meanings.

1 This is our main crop.
2 Hibernation is not how we deal with the cold.
3 We had a very poor harvest.
4 Another important factor is the equipment.
5 Fortunately we rarely have problems with the rivers.
6 We have many sorts of different things.
7 This is a trap, if you ask me.
8 They live and feed off other animals.
9 I ruined my argument by shouting.
10 Why don't you buzz off?
11 We were all stung several times.
12 They don't believe in the use of pesticides.

a We call them parasites.
b They farm organically.
c Just go away.
d We have a huge variety.
e We don't sleep during winter.
f That weakened what I said.
g The bees attacked us.
h We grow a lot of corn and almost nothing else.
i The area isn't prone to flooding.
j The weather damaged everything.
k It's not what it looks like.
l In addition, we have the right stuff.

11 Words and phrases ➜ *(pp. 59–60)*

1 My trousers are too tight – they must have __________ when I washed them. __________

2 They say small people __________ for their size by being aggressive. __________

3 It's __________ that many people don't want to __________ to society. __________

4 Our chickens _____ about 20 eggs a day. __________

5 It took me a while to __________ from the shock. __________

6 I always buy two of everything to __________ my __________ don't run out. __________

7 I always have __________ for breakfast. It's healthy. __________

8 What you said is just not __________. It doesn't make sense. __________

9 It's important that power __________ is reliable in all situations. __________

10 In a plane, it is the __________ who has the __________ responsibility for safety. __________

11 We always test the __________ of all our products. __________

12 Global warming will lead to the __________ of many animal species. __________

13 Our teacher told us that the _______ of our class is the highest in the school. __________

14 I could never eat a _______ _______, not even if it was __________. __________

Aussterben • beitragen • beunruhigend • Bio- • Eisbär • Erzeugung • Gesamt- • kompensieren • legen • logisch • Müsli • Pilot/in • schrumpfen • sich erholen • sicherstellen • Stand • Vorrat • Wirksamkeit

12 That's wrong!

Circle and correct the mistakes. Two sentences are correct.

1 The best type of breakfast for me is organnic muesli. __________

2 The dissappearance of plant species is very worying. __________

3 To insure our chickens lied a lot of eggs, we played them music. __________

4 The manager is in charge of the overal effektiveness of the process. __________

5 Our main priority for the future is the reliable generation of green power. __________

6 Many people say the power of the government shrunk last year. __________

7 Poler bear numbers are not recoverring; they're getting worse. __________

8 There is a logic connection between sea levells and global warming. __________

9 I have read feature articles on a variety of related topics. __________

10 I think it's important that everyone contributs to society in some way. __________

13 Words and phrases ➜ (pp. 61–64)

1 Say it ______________: no one has time to read ________ texts.	______________
2 He gave a ________ explanation of the ________ of the problem.	______________
3 The ________ is not just made up of TV ________!	______________
4 My favourite writer has a great ______________: his stories are so clever.	______________
5 When the company went ____________, she lost her job as a ________.	______________
6 ____________ like ______________ when they are at the supermarket.	______________
7 Thinking about ______________ situations is good for the imagination.	______________
8 Don't cross the road at a ________. It's dangerous.	______________
9 We looked down the ________ drop from the side of the mountain.	______________
10 ____________ has developed because people are ________.	______________
11 In some countries the ________ of men to women is very uneven.	______________
12 After school a ________ of 15 to 20 school children walked to the shopping mall.	______________
13 They say only mad people dream of ________ the world.	______________

Alternative • Auswirkung • bankrott • beherrschen • Bogen • Büroangestellte • Fantasie • Gang • hypothetisch • knapp • Kunde/Kundin • langatmig • Öffentlichkeit • schlau • senkrecht • sparsam • Verhältnis • Zivilisation • Zuschauer/in

14 Missing!

Add the missing part of the words.

1 When her business failed, she was declared __________**kr**__________.

2 We know coal is bad and won't last for ever, which is why we are looking for __________**nat**__________.

3 This isn't a real problem. It's a __________**the**__________. situation.

4 For this homework, I want you to use your __________**gin**__________. to write a science fiction story.

5 Unfortunately, the history of our __________**ili**__________. is also the story of regular wars between nations.

6 It is impossible to deny the huge __________**pa**__________. the computer has had on the world of work.

7 I'd much rather be playing a sport than to be a __________**tat**__________. watching from the side.

8 Have you heard the saying they use in business: "The __________**tom**__________. is always right"?

9 There's almost nothing to eat at home. I'm going into town to get some __________**pl**__________.

10 It's not only green, it also makes good financial sense to use resources __________**mi**__________.

15 Words and phrases ➜ (p. 65)

1 Artists achieve a sort of ________________ through their work.	________________
2 The way he ________ is – how shall I _____ it? – disgusting!	________________
3 We have worked hard and __________________ a lot.	________________
4 She said the painting was ____________ after she'd __________ ___ it.	________________
5 He _________________ the chairs to try to make the room seem tidier …	________________
6 … but the room still looked like a _______ had hit it.	________________
7 _________ is a big risk of smoking.	________________
8 There is ___________ an __________ between his work and Picasso!	________________
9 Yes, I am _____________ old and weak, but I still have strong opinions.	________________
10 The room is grey, but with some colourful ___________ for contrast.	________________
11 Careful! One of the legs on the table is a bit _______.	________________
12 You don't need __________ to enjoy a bit of ___________.	________________
13 I would never think of that. The idea would never _______ ___ me.	________________
14 We all have to learn to ignore our negative __________ ______________.	________________
15 I've seen my favourite film at least a ________ times.	________________

bezaubernd • einen Blick werfen auf • Bombe • Dutzend • jm. einfallen • erreichen • formulieren • gerade rücken • innerer Monolog • kauen • Kissen • körperlich • Krebs • locker • möglicherweise • Privatsphäre • romantische Liebe • Unsterblichkeit • Vergleich

16 The right word

Circle the correct word to complete the sentences.

1 What you said can't **possible • possibility • possibly** be correct.
2 She got up, checked her hair, **straight • straighten • straightened** her dress and left.
3 We might as well try this. After all, what have we got to **lose • loose • lost** ?
4 What people do in the **private • privacy • privately** of their own homes is their business.
5 He's a silent type. I think he finds it hard to put his **feels • feelings • feeling** into words.
6 My boyfriend sometimes buys me flowers: **romance • romantic • romantically** is not dead!
7 Only after the meeting did it **occur • occurrence • occurring** to me that the facts were wrong.
8 We have to learn to control the voice in our head, our own **inside • interior • inner** monologue.
9 The speech he gave only lasted two minutes. He's not a **word • wordy • words** person.
10 As a result of the strike, chaos **rule • ruler • rules** in the capital.

17 Words and phrases ➜ *(pp. 66–69)*

1 "I think our demands are ______," he said with great ______.	______
2 It's Donald's ______ opinion that he is extremely ______.	______
3 He swore ______ his breath as he ______ ______ after a difficult phone call.	______
4 The city of Bath got its name from hot ______ that were found there.	______
5 I had ______ the wrong number, so I made an ______ and said sorry.	______
6 They never ______ to say how ______ the area where they live is.	______
7 ______ is not what it was. I ______ it will continue to change.	______
8 The US wants a good trade relationship; China ______.	______
9 We all chose this ______, so you have nothing to ______ about.	______
10 The ______ is that we make ______ based on what we see and hear.	______

auflegen • ebenso • ehrlich • Entschuldigung • Ernsthaftigkeit • exklusiv • klug • Netzetikette • Quelle • Richtung • (Schluss-)Folgerung • sich beklagen • unterhalb (von) • vernünftig • vorhersagen • wählen • das Wesentliche • zögern

18 Scrambled sentences

Put the parts in the correct order.
The first one has been done for you.

a Change is a constant fact of life on earth, but few people would deny that the speed

b of technology, which has,revolutionised fields as varied as entertainment, medicine and

c the globe and improve effectiveness in many areas. What was before only possible in science

d harvests to feed our growing population. Our survival may depend on such applications of technology.

e about how we depend on our mobile phones and that our obsession with all things digital now

f robots and drones can work in harmony with nature in agriculture to ensure better

g business. While many people are uncomfortable with change in general, and complain

h rules the lives of millions, it is my sincere belief that the benefits far outweigh the

i before. To a large extent, this can be explained by the role in everyday life of our use

j risks. I predict technological progress will continue to create innovations that shrink

k fiction is now a vision of the future that our imagination can make a reality. Automation,

l of change in the past few years has been unlike anything we have witnessed

Answer: a ☐ ☐ ☐ ☐ ☐ ☐ ☐ ☐ ☐ ☐ ☐

19 Words and phrases ➜ (pp. 69–70)

1 From his clothes, I ___________ that he was quite rich.	___________
2 They are in love. They _____ _______ ____ get married soon.	___________
3 I ___________ said that you should not touch anything!	___________
4 I don't _______ him or think his ___________ of the film is genuine.	___________
5 I don't _________ him. That doesn't mean I have any ___________ for him.	___________
6 He was a cold person, and he rarely showed any ___________ for his children.	___________
7 The person who ________ the meeting normally acts as a ___________.	___________
8 The referee made a number of ___________ decisions during the match.	___________
9 A lot of people are ___________ new sources of energy.	___________
10 Do you think it's right to _____ people from wearing bikinis in public?	___________
11 Global warming is something that ___________ everyone.	___________
12 Parents shouldn't _______ _______ between their children.	___________
13 I ________ believe that the future can be bright if we do the right things now.	___________
14 Your work is always ___________ and well presented.	___________
15 You should show you are aware of ___________ to your beliefs.	___________

angehen • ausdrücklich • bewundern • Bewunderung • den Vorsitz führen • Gegenargument • gründlich • Missachtung • Moderator/in • nachdrücklich • Partei ergreifen • recherchieren • schließen • umstritten • verbieten • vertrauen • wahrscheinlich • Zuneigung

20 Two out of three

Add the missing words to two of the three gaps in these sentences.

1 I wouldn't trust ______ anything he says, if I were ______; he's prone ______ exaggerate things.

2 I don't want to ______ sides, but you are likely ______ find that both camps ______ have made good points.

3 How do you deal ______ families where ______ parents have lost ______ jobs as a result of automation?

4 I hesitate ______ say that robots pose ______ threat to our survival, but that's what ______ some believe.

5 We know, ______ instance, survival rates of ______ people recovering ______ cancer have improved a lot.

6 I admire the thorough way you researched the issues ______ concerning explicitly banning the use of mobiles in class.

7 She's experienced ______. She's been a moderator, and ______ addition she's chaired dozens ______ meetings.

8 You don't hang ______ when someone ______ talking. Similarly, netiquette ______ concerns online behaviour.

21 Quiz time!

1 Dogs, cats and snakes bite. What do bees do? ____________

2 Many people have an allergy to this. It makes them sneeze in summer. ____________

3 Water is liquid. It can also be a solid (ice). As a gas, it is … ____________

4 You should do this to the food you eat before you swallow it. ____________

5 This is something added to a chair to sit on for extra comfort. ____________

6 The opposite of horizontal. ____________

7 This is a line that is not straight. ____________

22 This person …

1 This person has a job that makes you laugh. ____________

2 This person sends a CV to a company, hoping for a job. ____________

3 This person travels and works in space. ____________

4 This person believes strongly in a cause, and actively supports it in public. ____________

5 This person has left their country and gone abroad to avoid war or persecution. ____________

6 This person was part of your family generations ago. ____________

7 This is someone who rides a bike. ____________

8 This is someone you don't want to meet. He or she breaks into houses to steal things. ____________

23 Mental training

Complete the words that end with -ment.

1 Don't walk in the road. Walk on the ____________ment.

2 She said she was innocent. She denied having any ____________ment in the crime.

3 My heart is beating so fast. The ____________ment is nearly unbearable.

4 If you want to do a job well, you need to have the right ____________ment.

5 I don't want to be late for my ____________ment with the doctor.

6 Nature needs our help. We have to look after the ____________ment.

7 The spectators couldn't believe their eyes. They watched in ____________ment.

8 If you do something wrong, you will get a ____________ment of some kind.